Mapping Motivation for Leadership

Mapping Motivation for Leadership, co-written with Jane Thomas, is the fourth of a series of seven books that are all linked to the author's Motivational Map toolkit. Each book builds on a different aspect of personal, team and organisational development.

This is a practical guide to leadership in the 21st century and builds on the '4+1' model outlined in the author's original book *Mapping Motivation: Unlocking the Key to Employee Energy and Engagement*. There is an increasing body of evidence, that the single most important aspect of being a leader relates to managing emotions effectively, and this management goes way beyond simply 'understanding' emotional intelligence; it is in fact a practice and one that is intimately connected with personal development and growth, and with energy. Energy, as *Mapping Motivation* made clear, is synonymous with motivation. The effective leaders of tomorrow will be those who understand their motivators, who regularly measure their motivators, sustain and replenish and maximise their motivators, and who do the same for their employees.

Clearly, there is a link here with the book on engagement, for leaders who do so will engage their employees. However, this book not only covers the motivational side of leadership, but also explores in detail the skill sets necessary in the '4+1' model: thinking skills, action skills, team skills and motivational skills plus that indefinable 'something' that is a commitment to personal development, so that we as leaders are not trying to solve today's problems with yesterday's training as our only internal resource.

James Sale is the Creative Director of Motivational Maps Ltd., a training company which he co-founded in 2006.

Jane Thomas is the Director of Premier Life Skills Ltd., a stress management and well-being training company.

The Complete Guide to Mapping Motivation

Motivation is the fuel that powers all our endeavours, whether they be individual, team or organisational. Without motivation we are bound to achieve far less than we really could, and without motivation we will fall short of what we are truly capable of. Motivation, before the creation by James Sale of Motivational Maps, has always been a 'flaky', subjective and impressionistic topic, and so-called 'motivational speakers' are perhaps rightly not considered entirely credible. But the Motivational Map has provided both language and metrics by which motivation can now be fully understood, described and utilised effectively. The Complete Guide to Mapping Motivation provides a total overview of how motivation informs all the critical activities that we and teams and organisations undertake at work. This includes how motivation is vital to the individual on a personal level if they want to be happy and fulfilled; it includes its applications in the domains of coaching, engagement, leadership, performance appraisal, team building and organisational development and change. So much has been written in the last 30 years about behaviours that often the literature has missed the crucial point: what drives the behaviours? This new model, then, instead of trying to control behaviours, seeks to understand motivators so that everyone can reach their full potential, not via command and control, but through bottom-up collaboration and appropriate reward strategies.

The Complete Guide to Mapping Motivation is a ground-breaking, innovative and new approach to managing motivation in the workplace. As such it is an essential series of books for all leaders, managers and key personnel engaged in improving how individuals, teams and whole organisations can be more effective, productive and engaged – and how they can want all of these things too.

Mapping Motivation for Engagement
James Sale and Steve Jones

Mapping Motivation for Leadership
James Sale and Jane Thomas

For more information about this series, please visit: www.routledge.com/The-Complete-Guide-to-Mapping-Motivation/book-series/MAPMOTIVAT

Mapping Motivation for Leadership

James Sale and Jane Thomas

Dear Barbara —
enjoy!
~ Sale
14 | 1 | 20

Routledge
Taylor & Francis Group

LONDON AND NEW YORK

First published 2020
by Routledge
2 Park Square, Milton Park, Abingdon, Oxon OX14 4RN

and by Routledge
52 Vanderbilt Avenue, New York, NY 10017

Routledge is an imprint of the Taylor & Francis Group, an informa business

© 2020 James Sale and Jane Thomas

Cover image "Moving Forward" by Linda E Sale
www.linda-sale-fine-art.com   lindaesale@gmail.com

Photo courtesy of the artist. Used with the artist's permission.

British Library Cataloguing in Publication Data
A catalogue record for this book is available from the British Library

Library of Congress Cataloging-in-Publication Data
Names: Sale, James, author.
Title: Mapping motivation for leadership / James Sale and Jane Thomas.
Description: 1 Edition. | New York, NY : Routledge, [2020] |
Series: The complete guide to mapping motivation | Includes index.
Identifiers: LCCN 2019012760| ISBN 9780815367567 (hardback) |
ISBN 9781351257046 (ebk)
Subjects: LCSH: Leadership--Psychological aspects. |
Motivation (Psychology)
Classification: LCC HD57.7 .S244 2020 | DDC 658.4/092--dc23
LC record available at https://lccn.loc.gov/2019012760

ISBN: 978-0-8153-6756-7 (hbk)
ISBN: 978-1-351-25704-6 (ebk)

Typeset in Times New Roman
by Taylor & Francis Books

MIX
Paper from
responsible sources
FSC™ C013985

Printed in the United Kingdom
by Henry Ling Limited

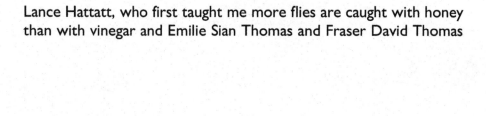

Lance Hattatt, who first taught me more flies are caught with honey than with vinegar and Emilie Sian Thomas and Fraser David Thomas

Contents

Figures

Acknowledgements

We would also like to thank all the licensees of Motivational Maps – nearly 500 worldwide; and especially our Senior Practitioners: Bevis Moynan, Carole Gaskell, Kate Turner, Susannah Brade-Waring and Heath Waring, who keep the flame full and burning.

Behind the scenes James Watson and Rob Breeds have provided invaluable support and advice and we are very grateful. Also, thanks go to my son, Joseph Sale, the writer and writing coach, who has strenuously promoted this series of books through his blogs and social media commentary.

Linda E Sale, the artist and Managing Director of Motivational Maps Ltd., has to be thanked for support and faith in the creation of this work so far reaching it cannot really be described; but what can be described is the fact that all the figures in this book, and the cover illustration too, are her work. We are truly grateful – and in awe of her abilities.

It is important, too, that we recognise the superb work of our Senior Routledge Editor, Kristina Abbotts, whose faith, confidence and help in this has been exceptional.

Series editor introduction
The Complete Guide to Mapping Motivation

Following the success of *Mapping Motivation*, a definitive text book on the topic of motivation, it was decided that there was a lot more to say about motivation, and which needed to be said! Motivation is the fuel that powers all our endeavours, whether they be individual, team or organisational. Without motivation we are bound to achieve far less than we really could, and without motivation we will fall short of what we are truly capable of.

Motivation, before the creation of Motivational Maps, has always been a 'flaky', subjective and impressionistic topic, and so-called 'motivational speakers' are perhaps rightly not considered entirely credible. But the Motivational Map has provided both language and metrics by which motivation can now be fully understood, described and utilised effectively. The Complete Guide to Mapping Motivation series provides a total overview of how motivation informs all the critical activities that we and teams and organisations undertake at work. This includes how motivation is vital to the individual on a personal level if they want to be happy and fulfilled; it includes its applications in the domains of coaching, engagement, leadership, performance appraisal, team building and organisational development and change.

So much has been written in the last 30 years about behaviours that often the literature has missed the crucial point: what drives the behaviours? This new model, then, instead of trying to control behaviours, seeks to understand motivators so that everyone can reach their full potential, not via Command and Control, but through bottom-up collaboration and appropriate reward strategies. The Complete Guide to Mapping Motivation series is a groundbreaking, innovative and new approach to managing motivation in the workplace. As such it is an essential series of books for all leaders, managers and key personnel engaged in improving how individuals, teams and whole organisations can be more effective, productive and engaged – and how they can want all of these things too.

James Sale, Series Editor

Preface

Mapping Motivation for Leadership is the fourth volume in the series, The Complete Guide to Mapping Motivation. Four is, in the sequence of 1 to 7 (the planned number for the series), exactly half-way, which seems appropriate given the importance of this topic: the application of motivation to the domain of leadership. Leadership is central to everything, full stop! It is almost impossible to think of anything more significant in life than this topic, since it – like motivation itself – pervades every area of it. We all want to know: who's in charge? Who's responsible, who's accountable? Indeed, this primacy of the question of leadership extends way beyond business and organisation; it saturates everything about our lives.

To take a simple but powerful example: consider religions. Perhaps the profoundest question (and there are many!) in the whole Bible is this one: "By what authority are You doing these things, and who gave You this authority?"[1] These are not the words of Jesus but of the Pharisees challenging Christ's apparent authority. We say apparent because we are not making a religious 'pitch' here – atheists, like the Pharisees, would reject (rightly or wrongly, which is not our issue in this book) the authority of Jesus, or of the Bible, or of a specific church. The point is, in rejecting these 'authorities', they accept others.[2] And the overarching point is: a leader has to have authority from somewhere in order to function at all, and we shall be looking at these kinds of authority in Chapter 1 and 5.

But if this is true at a religious level, so it is true at a political, social and even domestic level. Somebody, usually, or some group[3] has authority, which is accepted, and so exerts leadership on others. It is important to say at this stage that leadership can be shared, and if we think politically it could be argued that democracy itself is a mechanism for enabling the sharing of authority over time. However, when we think of most organisations and businesses that we know and which are successful, there is invariably a strong leadership that centres on a person, which creates a hierarchy below him or her, and in which hierarchy members may or may not be authorised or empowered to lead at their respective levels.

The word leadership comes from the verb to lead, and etymologically seems related to old Teutonic or old English words meaning road or journey, or to go or to travel. In other words, the common sense essence of what leadership is about is helping others (and an organisation or a country, as an entity) get from A to B. We appoint a new leader when the old one steps down, retires, is fired or dies, and we think: currently, we are *here*, but in fact we can't stay *here*, because if we do, we will die;[4] so we need somebody to help us get to *there*. Often in business, getting to *there* simply means something like quadrupling profitability, but as we shall see that would be a very limited view of what a true leader can and should achieve.

In Chapter 8 of our first book *Mapping Motivation* we specifically touch on the connection between leadership and motivation, and provide a general outline of the model that we use. This model is the '4+1' model; and what we have sketched before, we are in this volume going to describe in much, much more detail. But the important fact that we established in that earlier volume was that if one considered leadership as properly, as effectively, understood then there was a much greater connection between it and motivation than was commonly accepted.[5] Indeed, we estimated that at least some 50% of leadership was really about motivation, and the mastery of motivation with oneself and other people; and furthermore, we made the point that this means that leadership is not the 'yang'[6] of business and organisational life that it is often made out to be, but more the 'yin'. There is always a balance between yin and yang, but yin precedes the yang, and it is yin which invariably overcomes the yang.

Another way of expressing what we are saying, but using more managerial jargon, is that soft skills are more important than hard ones when we consider true leadership. This is certainly proverbially true. We learn from wisdom literature that "a soft answer turneth away wrath",[7] from folklore that we 'catch more flies with honey than with vinegar',[8] and from the Tao Te Ching, "the soft wins victory over the hard".[9] Everywhere we look where serious enquirers have considered human activities and what constitutes success, we find that there is an emphasis on the more invisible, intangible, 'softer', some might say more feminine, skills that trump the more overt, tangible, aggressive and masculine attributes that traditionally have been exalted as the very essence of real leadership.

This distinction is an important point because what it means is that what we are going through in the twenty-first century is a radical re-formation or transformation of what it means to be an effective leader. We have to get away from the old, traditional model because – frankly – it isn't working very well, and is no longer ideologically acceptable. And if we need a new model of leadership, and if, as we already established in our earlier book, some 50% of more of good leadership is about motivation, then clearly we have to understand motivation at a much deeper level than we have heretofore. For, as has been observed, "So, if my inner motivation is wrong, then I will create the effects of that wrong motivation".[10] Consequences, then, follow from wrong motivation – the invisible – in the outside world, the visible. But it all starts inside.

Leadership[11] and motivation, therefore, are of critical importance in the success of any organisation. Leadership is instrumentally involved in all three dimensions of performance: it has a critical role to play in setting the direction of an organisation; it necessarily must ensure ongoing learning, knowledge acquisition and upskilling of employees; and it certainly must seek to fuel the motivations of all its staff, so that there is a real desire to carry on and achieve worthwhile goals. Failure to do any of these three things will lead to failure in the long term. But just as we need a new model of leadership, which this book explores, so we need a correspondingly new model of motivation: one that can describe, measure, monitor and maximise this essential ingredient in our lives and working lives. This is where Motivational Maps comes in.

In one sense the creation of Motivational Maps is one aspect of this new model for leadership that the twenty-first century needs. Our view would be that the Personality tests and tools that arose after World War Two were Generation One of the serious attempts to get inside what makes an employee tick; but they had limitations. So subsequently, Generation Two, a wave of Psychometric tools developed which enabled a wider sweep (but which still included personality) of qualities to be assessed. One advantage of the psychometric was its arduous validation process whereby its measures to be valid were compared to a representative sample of the population at least twice.[12] This was and is all well and good, except the net effect of it has been to disempower leadership in two ways: first, the very fact that the psychometric requires (in the second testing) for the subject to be consistent actually tends to hypostatise the person – or put another way, 'fix' or stereotype them. Which leads to the second problem: leaders instead of employing engaging managers and able leaders based on a range of criteria – critically motivation should be one of them – tend to look for the simple and simplistic solution of the 'right' psychometric profile.[13]

And that is why Motivational Maps as a Third Generation tool is really the right idea at the right time, for in yet another important way it does what the other tools do not: namely, it reverses the flow of management focus. What do we mean by that exactly? Well, Personality and Psychometric tools operate on a top-down approach: it invariably seems to be about finding out whether the employee fits the manager's box. Top-down or Command and Control[14] in other words. Motivational Maps cannot and does not work like that: the essence of doing a Motivational Map is to understand the employee in order for the management or the leadership to accommodate the employee, not the other way round. In short, it is a bottom-up approach, a people-centric approach, an engagement approach. This approach does three important things: it increases productivity because it increases motivation and participation, it thus anticipates customer needs more quickly and readily, and it facilitates greater innovation[15] because of the greater involvement of employees. All vital in the twenty-first century economy; and, beneficially, all likely to enhance personal well-being as well as organisational profits. And, of course, these are all things that the leader wishes to achieve. Indeed, ideally, as it says in the Tao Te Ching: "If a wholly Great One rules, the people hardly know that he exists".[16] In other words, the work has been accomplished, but the leader's ego has been left behind or never surfaced.

This work is a standalone, although it builds on the foundation of *Mapping Motivation*,[17] the primary source book, and of *Mapping Motivation for Coaching*,[18] and *Mapping Motivation for Engagement*, its two sequels. We have tried to keep repetition of materials to a minimum, so that readers of this work, if they enjoy it, will definitely like the former texts and derive enormous benefit from them. To help get the reader up to speed as quickly as possible, each book in the new *Complete Guide to Mapping Motivation* series will contain a brief introductory and summary chapter explaining the basics of Motivational Maps; this will be distilled from *Mapping Motivation*. This overview of the Motivational Maps' structure and meaning should enable any reader to be able to understand pretty quickly what this is all about.

There are powerful ideas to be found here, as well as transformative techniques and tools to be deployed; some can be used in an isolated and one-off kind of way, others can be used in combination, and still more others require Motivational Map technology. But we are not prescriptive; on the contrary, pragmatism rules – will it work for you? If so, use it. At the end of the day we all need to understand that management and psychological models are not reality:[19] they are a map of reality, and all maps suffer from the deficiency of being incomplete to a greater or lesser extent. As it happens, Motivational Maps, as a model, is extremely accurate,[20] and the results it produces at the individual, team and organisational level have been nothing short of astonishing and revelatory to those concerned. We hope that you, too, will enjoy a similar sense of astonishment and revelation as you read through this work – and ultimately will want to become more involved.

Underpinning it all, then, is the Motivational Map, which we give full access to in this Endnote.[21] You may wish to go there immediately in order to activate your personal Motivational Map as a prelude to reading this book. Certainly, the contents will make even more sense to you if you do.

This leads on to one final point in this Preface: namely, that this book has not been written in a strictly sequential way, but rather topologically; it is entirely possible to dip in and out of it as one's interests dictate. Basically, we use the '4+1' model as the template around which we thread Map applications and what we consider to be simple but in-depth ideas that help generate better, more informed and more effective leadership. But as you will see, leadership – like this book – is a tapestry: there are many threads and they interconnect and interact with each other. So you will find thematic threads –

especially of self-awareness and engaging teams – continually cropping up and not only located in their specific chapters. Go ahead – read, explore, enjoy, and focus on motivation, for it will enhance your leadership.

Notes

1 Matthew's gospel, 21 v.23, *New American Standard Bible*, AJ Holman (1973).
2 The writings of David Hume, Karl Marx, Richard Dawkins, for example; or, say, a materialistic interpretation of 'science'.
3 The Quakers, for example, do not have individual leaders in their 'diffused' model, but a process by which the collective will of the membership is 'discerned' and then acted upon.
4 "For things to remain the same, everything must change" – a translation from the Italian of Giuseppe Tomasi Di Lampedusa's famous novel, *The Leopard*.
5 For example, in Adrian Furnham's otherwise excellent and exhaustive, *The Psychology of Behaviour at Work*, Psychology Press (2005), we have a whole chapter devoted to leadership: 41 pages reviewing all the literature and theories about leadership. But the verb 'motivate' doesn't appear until four pages in, and thereafter it hardly features prominently at all. It is curious how academics fail to see its centrality, and yet any true leader understands its necessity in the real world of leading.
6 "Yin and yang are ... the starting point for change. When something is whole, by definition, it's unchanging and complete. So when you split something into two halves – yin/yang, it upsets the equilibrium of wholeness. Both halves are chasing after each other as they seek a new balance with each other. The word Yin comes out to mean "shady side" and Yang "sunny side". Yin Yang is the concept of duality forming a whole. We encounter examples of Yin and Yang every day. As examples: night (Yin) and day (Yang), female (Yin) and male (Yang). Over thousands of years, quite a bit has been sorted and grouped under various Yin Yang classification systems" – https://bit.ly/2kz6XJ6.
7 Proverbs Chapter 15 v. 1. King James Bible.
8 For more information on the proverb, go to – https://bit.ly/2sk39im.
9 Lao Tzu, Tao Te Ching, 36, Richard Wilhelm edition. Also, from section 43, "The softest thing on earth overtakes the hardest thing on earth" and "Everyone on earth knows that the weak conquers the strong and the soft conquers the hard – but no-one is capable of acting accordingly" from section 77.
10 Attributed to C. McGeachy.
11 Indeed, almost certainly the number 1 factor, without which all other good things – for example, a great product, a positive culture, powerful marketing – tend to fail.
12 See Cindy Boisvert – https://bit.ly/2qw0ySr.
13 Lest this be thought fanciful, consider Paul Flowers, the once Chair of the Co-operative Banking Group (and who nearly destroyed the Bank) and who was described by the UK Government's Treasury committee chairman Andrew Tyrie, in this way: Flowers proved to be "psychologically unbalanced but psychometrically brilliant". For more on this see: James Sale – https://bit.ly/2H4YneP.
14 Of course, as we say about Maps more generally, context is everything: there are situations (often very high risk and dangerous) where Command and Control is the best way to manage a situation or event. That said, however, in modern democracies this approach for day-to-day work and business is increasingly seen as authoritarian and ineffective.

15 "Trust me, your employees are exercising their creativity somewhere, it just may not be at work" – Gary Hamel, *The Future of Management*, Harvard Business School Press (2007). This is what effective leadership reverses.
16 Lao Tzu, Tao Te Ching, 17, Richard Wilhelm edition.
17 *Mapping Motivation*, James Sale, Gower (2016).
18 *Mapping Motivation for Coaching*, James Sale and Bevis Moynan, Routledge (2018).
19 "A map is not the territory it represents, but, if correct, it has a similar structure to the territory, which accounts for its usefulness" – Alfred Korzybski, *Science and Sanity* (1933). This expression subsequently became a major principle underpinning Neuro Linguistic Programming (NLP), whose application we consider in much more detail in Chapter 4 of this book.
20 For example, Face Validity testing – which asks users of the Motivational Map to rate its accuracy – records a 95% accuracy rating.
21 To obtain a link to do a complimentary Motivational Map, send an email to info@motivationalmaps.com and put the word LEADERMAP in the heading.

Introduction to *Mapping Motivation for Leadership*

Leadership is a truly difficult topic to write or even think about. As Adrian Furnham puts it: "The topic of leadership is one of the oldest areas of research in the social sciences, yet one of the most problematic".[1] It is problematic for many reasons, including, on the one hand, our over-familiarity with the topic because we are exposed to leadership constantly,[2] and so we think we know something about it. This is much the same as thinking we know something about education because we went to school once upon a time; of course, we may actually know something, but chances are we have a superficial, partial and stereotypical view of the subject. On the other hand, the essential ambiguity of leadership, and how leaders function, shifts, as values shift, and what seems to work in one context may not in another.[3] Add to that the fact that the social sciences which like to study the matter, are not like the hard sciences: it is difficult if not impossible to run double-blind experiments where we get unassailable results. And to top it all, historically (and which relates to the shifting values we mentioned), we find even as we write this in the UK that there is a movement afoot which seeks to have removed the statues of Churchill and Nelson[4] in London on the grounds that they were not the great leaders the British people have always thought they were, but oppressors and racists.

What, then, is leadership, true leadership? Whatever it is, we at Motivational Maps, know one thing: leaders produce real success for all the stakeholders, and "only what is simple can produce outstanding success".[5] We mention this because we do need in this Introduction to give a brief overview of the academic theories surrounding leadership, but we also need to say that whilst there is always something to learn from all of these theories it is important to keep at the forefront of one's thinking the imperative that only simple things[6] work in leadership and management. Maps – theories – are not the territory; they are simply guides and pointers. A common sense approach is in order.

There seems to be four main theories of what leadership is about: trait, behavioural, contingency, and attributional.

Trait theories attempt to identify the characteristics of leaders: is there a common set of specific traits that all great leaders have? Today this type is still with us, though the model has been largely discredited. We see this in all the literature about the 'great' leaders and books about how to be like them. But the problem is, as Nelson is finding out, one day you are a hero, the next a villain: take 'Sir' Fred Goodwin, Philip Green, and Jack Welch as three good examples. At one point in their respective careers, it seemed there could not be enough stories about their magical leadership abilities – and how everyone else could be like them. Sadly, however, their credibility was shredded by events of their own making.

Nevertheless, whilst there is no final and agreed set of traits[7] all leaders have, it is useful to think about the 20% of core ones without which leadership cannot be leadership. Leaders, for example, must spend a lot of time in, and being comfortable with, the future, for unless they are seeing a future for their organisation, how can they lead anyone else there? Clearly, too, persistence and resilience are crucial, else they would fall by the wayside. Then, again, energy and influence are critical; and for energy let us substitute our favourite word: motivation. Finally, integrity is essential for without it – as some heroes who have fallen from favour found – the other traits get undermined.[8]

Behavioural theories, given that an agreed set of traits cannot be found, focus on preferable leadership actions. What do good leaders do? Such behaviours, it is argued, can be developed by training. Two dimensions of behaviour that much research was invested in were initiating structure and consideration. Leaders who were 'high' in initiating structure were extremely task orientated – concerned about their staff getting the job done, having clear responsibilities, and meeting deadlines and so on. Those who were 'high' in consideration had a strong focus on the relationships aspect of their work – trust, mutual respect, regard would all be critical factors in the work environment. But Behavioural theories ran into the same problems as trait: namely, identifying a common set of behaviours that were universally applicable was found difficult.[9]

Despite insights, both theories – sometimes thought of as one and two dimensional – were found inadequate. Contingency theory attempted to identify situational variables that would influence outcomes. The key aspect of this work is to consider how one leadership approach whilst being relevant and successful in one situation, becomes invalid in another. In other words – and as the description 'situational' suggests – leadership all depends on finding the appropriate style to match the actual condition that is being encountered.

The kind of variables that contingency likes to consider as making a difference to leadership outcomes are: degree of structure in the task, the quality of relationships between the leader and staff, the leader's position power, environment, staff's role clarity, group norms, information availability, staff acceptance of leader's decisions, staff maturity.

The first four of these variables have been thought particularly important. But one can see that if, as in the Behavioural model, two dimensions (task and people orientation) can produce 81 classifications, then an incomplete list of nine variables has scope for producing a great deal more. Contingency theories increasingly become complex and divorced from common sense. This makes them difficult to apply in practical situations. That said, they have produced interesting insights into how leadership can be more effective, and furthermore it does seem *common sense* that different situations do require different leadership styles.[10]

Finally, Attribution theory[11] addresses the difficulties of situational analysis by suggesting that leadership is what people characterise leaders as having. This, then, is a perceptual view of leadership – its interpretation hinges on what people perceive as 'real'. So, for example, people characterise effective leaders as being consistent. The immediate advantage of this approach is its common sense: it rings a chord precisely because it registers how people think about leaders. In this way it almost takes us full circle to trait theories, because they seem self-evident too. Trait predicates people as having the qualities; attribution theory predicates that people perceive leaders as having particular qualities: so, for example, leaders may be perceived as having intelligence, strong personalities, verbal skills, aggressiveness, industriousness, and so on. More specifically, charismatic leaders are often identified as having these qualities: self-confidence, vision, articulation of vision, strong convictions about the vision, novel behaviour, perceptions of them as change agents – that is what they do, environmental sensitivity, etc.

These, then, are four of the leading theories; we, however, are pragmatic about this. We like 'things' that work, and ideas based on observation and experience; and so we like a distinction that emerged in the twentieth century[12] between what has been called transformational leadership,[13] and this is usually contrasted with transactional leadership:

> Transformational leadership serves to enhance the motivation, morale, and job performance of followers through a variety of mechanisms; these include connecting the follower's sense of identity and self to a project and to the collective identity of the organization; being a role model for followers in order to inspire them and to raise their interest in the project; challenging followers to take greater ownership for their work, and understanding the strengths and weaknesses of followers, allowing the leader to align followers with tasks that enhance their performance.[14]

Clearly, this is so resonant to us and what we do because the first quality that such leaders have is that they 'enhance the motivation'; motivation is centre stage in this leadership model, as it should be.

Before going on to consider motivation, let's briefly review the differences between transformational and transactional. The best way, perhaps, of grasping these concepts is by way of juxtaposing them in terms of the distinction between leadership per se and management. Put another way, transactional leadership tends to be viewed as the kind of leadership that 'manages' an organisation. Thus it tends to:

- plan to meet current objectives
- use resources efficiently
- manage current problems
- focus on processes working well
- ensure people work to contract
- seek improvements through training
- establish standard procedures
- focus on efficiency
- and generally have a present time orientation.

Thus, this is about ensuring that the resources we have – the people – are efficiently deployed, and so the emphasis is on processes and systems. On the other hand, transformational leadership is more concerned with:

- long-term vision
- broad purposes
- creating a better future (so value-laden)
- focus on the quality of service provided
- inspiring, leading by example and encouragement
- creating more effective systems, focusing on effectiveness
- and finally having a future time orientation.

This kind of leadership is more concerned with effectiveness, and so the emphasis tends to be more on results and outcomes. One neat way of expressing this is: transactional leaders tend to 'do things right', whereas transformational leaders tend to 'do the right things'.[15] But 'to do the right things' is quite different from 'doing things right': the latter has very little moral or value content, but the former is inevitably – with its future orientation – value-driven and moral; for the transformational leader wishes to improve 'things', including potentially the world, by their activities. And so leadership in this incarnation is a high calling.

With this overview in place, let us return to where this book is going. Already we have said that only simple things work. In *Mapping Motivation*[16] we outlined what we called our '4+1' model of leadership. The essence of this model is that there are four key skills, and these skills can be taught; there is hope therefore that anyone can improve as a leader if they develop one or any of these four skills. These skills, as our chapters are going to reveal, are wide-ranging, but nevertheless they lead to the practice of new behaviours, and new levels of performance. But the '+1' is not a skill, as we are going to see; it is a quality of mind, an attitude of being, a commitment of the heart that makes it much more intangible, invisible, than any skill or behaviour. Its subtlety means that it can easily be lost or overlooked; and worse, means it can easily be faked too. As the profound business philosopher, Chin-Ning Chu, observed: 'They can read and understand a thousand times, but the idea never really becomes a part of them'.[17]

We are perhaps too familiar with this problem in the workplace: people who are 'qualified', even overqualified, and yet cannot successfully perform in the domain where their qualifications indicate they would, or should. There is a more widespread issue here which is worth commenting on since this book is about leadership: that is, the tendency that we have frequently observed of people being drawn to professions, activities and titles for which they are peculiarly unsuited. Indeed, in Chapter 7 we study just such an individual in some detail. It's as if at some subconscious level they know they are deficient in a specific area, and something in them drives them to work in that very field to show others that they are competent and capable; in short, to compensate in some way, though of course it means avoiding one's true path and purpose. So, for example, one meets teachers who have no understanding or empathy with young people, much less a desire to develop them; one encounters social workers who are no more psychologically integrated than the clients they work with; one discovers artists with no more ability to paint than a student in lower school (but plenty of vaulting ambition to be *an artist*); and one spots in all kinds of organisations individuals with MBAs, PhDs, Fellowships in any number of prestigious managerial associations but who are the most detested and avoided managers or leaders within a five-mile radius of their presence! Being upskilled, then, isn't the key issue, because individuals can have all the training in the world, and have certificates to prove it, but still be nowhere near the mark that constitutes real performance as a leader. Something else is necessary: something connected with our '+1'.

And so a further issue is that this '+1' is, counter intuitively, far more important than the four skills;[18] it is the foundation, the bed rock, and all the skills in the world are no substitute for it. So we will be devoting two whole chapters to exploring '+1' and how we approach it, see it, and develop it.

The '4+1' model briefly, then, is a follows. There are four key skills that leaders have to master and they are: thinking, doing, team building and motivating. These are our simple, homely terms for the four skills sets, but as we shall see when we unpack them, each one of them is exceedingly dense and rich. The '+1' is the profound attribute of self-awareness[19] leading to self-growth: the kind of mind-set that perpetually self-examines and takes action on its own feedback loop.[20]

Superimposed on all elements of leadership is the spirit of motivation. It remains then to say in this Introduction why this is so important. In the first instance, motivation is energy and without it nothing can or will be done. One theme we will doubtless be returning to many times is the motivation of the leader, which must always be higher than that of the team members. Why? Because, followers take their cue from leaders, and will adjust their own motivations to that which they find in their leader. So, if the leader is poorly motivated, their own employees – over time – will become just the same. This means a loss of performance and a drop in productivity.

Second, actually, leadership and motivation are exceedingly similar in at least the sense that they are both ambiguous. This is hardly surprising, given that we claim some 50% or more of leadership concerns motivational issues. But as we wrestle with the ambiguity of motivation we are making a huge step forward in helping to resolve some of the ambiguities of leadership. To be more specific: our fourth skill is 'motivating' and by this we mean most essentially one's immediate reports; this is very much a one-to-one kind of motivation. How does one do that? Clearly, being motivated by oneself is necessary but not sufficient to accomplish this; and here is where Motivation Maps come in, and the process of mapping motivations, since this at last provides some clarity as to what motivation is, how to describe it, measure, monitor and maximise it. The tool opens up a whole new way of looking at this issue.

Third, motivation cuts across not just the one-to-one issues, but clearly is vital to team building, our third skill, and also 'Doing', the second skill. There are several areas where this is true, but of utmost importance in the role of a leader is the 'doing' of recruitment: leaders have to recruit highly motivated individuals, but how do they do that? Mapping Motivation can show how and provide a leading edge over other methods.

Finally, and even in the most unlikely place, 'Thinking', motivation has its part to play. Over and above whether or not one is motivated to 'think' at all, 'thinking' is sometimes considered the quintessential component of what leadership does, for it is the job of the leader to consider – to think about – the future. Whereas other employees can get on with their jobs and roles in the present, the leader *must* think about the future. Some posher words we often use to describe this is that they 'envision' what is to be, and that they 'strategize' how they will get there. Business plans need ultimately to be products of such thinking. But here's the thing: when we consider organisational change some seem to think they can do it without reference to their people at all! We generate a plan and command them to do it – whether they like it or not; we fire them if they don't do what we say. This is the traditional top-down method then. But what if we take a totally different approach, a more bottom-up approach? What if we are fully aware of employee motivational drivers, all of them, and what if we align our mission and our vision with those motivational profiles? In other words, the motivators drive the changes? If that were to happen, then, we would be in a situation where we could truly say that motivation has become a strategic issue[21] for any organisation; and so any leader, worth their salt, would need to be an expert in motivation, for everything would depend upon it.

This is the ultimate goal of the leader, for if we had it the productivity and creativity unleashed would generate a power that would make the organisation virtually unstoppable, and who would be able to compete? No-one, apart from the organisation that did the same. But here too is an interesting corollary: what are the chances that, even if another organisation replicated the methodology we are advocating, that they would end up in the same place? Actually, not at all. Why? Because the motivational profile driving such change would likely be very different, and so the vision, mission and strategies emerging would be entirely different too. In such a scenario, one is much less likely to be competing rather than creating one's own unique marketplace where one's position is pre-eminent.

And arriving at the word 'pre-eminent' we are exactly where we need to be when we talk of leadership, for to be 'pre-eminent' is to be number one, a star, a winner. This is not just for themselves: it is for those they lead. Their organisations, their companies, their teams, all become leaders in their field. In this way the organisation realises its full potential, just as the leader does. Warren Bennis put it this way: "Becoming a leader is synonymous with becoming yourself. It is precisely that simple, and it is also that difficult".[22] And so with the organisation; it becomes itself, its full self.

With these thoughts in mind, then, it is time to enter the wonderful and ambiguous world of motivation and leadership, and to consider many aspects of the '4+1' model over the next eight chapters. It will help you massively if you have done a Motivational Map and used the code given in endnote 21 of the Preface to this volume. Further, we also in the next section provide a summary of Motivational Maps, so you can quickly get up to speed with the ideas around this concept, and this will enable the chapters to make even more sense more readily.

Notes

1 Adrian Furnham, *The Psychology of Behaviour at Work*, Psychology Press (2005).
2 Via our politicians, priests, jobs, families, community centres and services, and just about anywhere we go we find that someone is in charge – someone is the leader.
3 As Professor Amin Rajan noted, "Like love, leadership is hard to define", *Professional Manager* issue 33, March 2002.
4 For example, see *The Guardian* article for a flavour of this development: https://bit.ly/2x7Yphn.
5 D G Krause, *The Way of the Leader*, Nicolas Brearley (1997).
6 Which is not, of course, to commit the mistake, which some leaders do, of always simplifying interpretations of data, so that the wrong problems are 'successfully' addressed. Only simple things work; but oversimplification of interpretations need to be carefully guarded against. In fact, this issue is one of five processes that Karl E Weick and Kathleen M Sutcliffe in their book, *Managing the Unexpected*, Wiley (2015) claim is a key trait of HROs: high reliability organisations.
7 The lack of an agreed set of traits is a difficulty for the theory; and it also highlights another issue which we will come to: if there are leadership traits, then do

men and women share them? What is the difference between male and female leadership styles?

8   Warren Buffett expressed this in a wonderful way: "You can't make a good deal with a bad person" – https://bit.ly/2TnGRsi.

9   Whilst behavioural theory did not produce a commonly accepted list of proven and preferable behaviours that would guarantee good leadership, it did create at least one useful tool for the analysis of leadership style: the so-called Blake and Mouton Managerial Grid. This effectively develops the notions of people versus task orientation and breaks them down to 81 possible combinations! A lot to consider. But self-awareness of where one stands in the continuum can be useful for a leader.

10 One particularly successful version of Contingency that has not been swamped with the difficulties of endless boxes, and has had wide application in the UK, is Adair's Action-Centred model of leadership. Adair posited that success in leadership depended upon effectiveness in three crucial areas: task needs (getting the job done), group needs (ensuring the group doing it works effectively and sustaining morale and motivation), individual needs (catering for individual needs and attempting to dovetail these with the needs of the task and of the group) – John Adair, *Effective Leadership*, Gower (1983), reprint Pan (1988).

11 For a more detailed account of all four theories, see James Sale, *Growing Leaders*, Courseware Publications (1998).

12 According to Wikipedia, which provides a very neat summary: "Transformational leadership is a style of leadership where a leader works with subordinates to identify needed change, creating a vision to guide the change through inspiration, and executing the change in tandem with committed members of a group" – https://bit.ly/2fonjTD.

13 A concept first introduced by James V Downton, and subsequently developed by leadership expert James MacGregor Burns. See Burns, *Transforming Leadership*, Grove Press (reprint 2004).

14 Wikipedia, ibid.

15 Peter F Drucker, *The Essential Drucker*, Taylor & Francis (2001).

16 James Sale, *Mapping Motivation*, Gower (2016).

17 Chin-Ning Chu, *Thick Face, Black Heart*, Nicolas Brearley (1997).

18 Another way of expressing this is, "Poor leadership largely derives from emotional deficiencies, not intellectual ones" – James Sale, *Growing Leaders*, Courseware Publications (1998).

19 "Great leaders are people who learn to know and control themselves before trying to control others" said a former head of recruitment for the famous SAS, quoted in the *Financial Times*, and cited in *The Week*, 9/11/96.

20 To get the sense of the importance of what we are saying here, consider this observation: "There is one quality that trumps all, evident in virtually every great entrepreneur, manager, and leader. That quality is self-awareness. The best thing leaders can do to improve their effectiveness is to become more aware of what motivates them and their decision-making" – Anthony Tjan, *Harvard Business Review*, cited by Ian Morgan Cron and Suzanne Stabile, *The Road Back to You: An Enneagram Journey to Self-Discovery*, IVP Books (2016).

21 We say this in our earlier book, "But if we now turn this round and start with Motivation as our corner stone, then we get a very different kind of organisation. Here, if we start with motivation, then we are starting with 'why' we do what we do; we are checking in on the hearts and minds of the individuals involved. Indeed, it asks us to be clear about our purpose, not some imposed, extraneous and arbitrary purpose (which usually means one uniform thing: making money, which is

not a purpose but a result), but a purpose – a 'why' – that is something intrinsic to us, and so deeply motivating. As Daniel Pink put it: motivation acts as a 'purpose maximiser'. The direction we are going in does not express our purpose, but tells us more about 'what' we are doing and where that leads us to (a result); our skills and knowledge manifestly tells us about 'how' we are doing what we are doing. But Simon Sinek said, " 'WHAT companies do are external factors, but WHY they do it is something deeper'; and that something deeper links to our motivators" – James Sale and Steve Jones, *Mapping Motivation for Engagement*, Routledge (2018).

22 Warren Bennis and Robert Townsend, *Reinventing Leadership*, Judy Piatkus (1996).

Summary of Motivational Maps
What you need to know in a nutshell!

Within each person there are nine motivators – we all have these motivators, and we all have the full nine; the difference is that each individual has the nine in a different order and at a different level of intensity. This gives rise to the possibility of millions of potential combinations in an individual's profile. Over 50,000 Maps have been completed and we still have never seen two individuals with identical Maps; furthermore, because motivation is partially based on our belief systems, it changes over time. It is not static and it is not fixed, and so it is impossible to stereotype anyone according to their motivators, since these will change. Usually, most people are directly influenced not by just their top motivator, but by their top 3 motivators; rarely, this can be their top two or top four, but the scoring shows what really counts or not (which are motivators scoring > 20).

Motivation is energy; it is what fuels us to do 'things' – things we want to do. Without motivation we are unlikely to set out in the direction we want to go (towards our goals) and are even more unlikely to use our knowledge and skills effectively. In short, motivation is the fuel in the tank of the car we call performance. Thus, knowing what motivates us and how to reward – or re-fuel – our motivators is to enable higher levels of energy, greater levels of performance and productivity, and to seriously increase our satisfaction with life.

The nine motivators are not random or discrete; but instead form a holistic unity. They are divided into three groups of three; the groups like the motivators themselves have properties as well as motivational qualities. Some motivators are aligned and reinforce each other; other motivators conflict and cause tension, whether that be at an individual (that is, internal), team or organisational level. The tension is not necessarily a bad thing; it can lead, for example, to procrastination – to taking longer to make a decision – but equally taking longer can sometimes mean making a better decision. In Motivational Maps, therefore, as an absolute rule, there is no good or bad profile: context determines the meaning of every profile.

So, to expand and summarise the key principles underpinning Motivational Maps, then there are nine:

1   All Map profiles are good. There are not good or bad profiles – the diagnostic is ipsative, which means that you are measuring yourself against yourself, so you cannot be 'wrong'. What you 'think' can be wrong but how you 'feel' cannot be: it is how you feel; and so it is with your motivation, as they are feeling-based.

2   Context is everything in interpreting Maps. There can be no one meaning isolated from the context in which the individual is operating. Profiles may suit or re-inforce a specific context or not; 'or not' may mean that intention (will power), knowledge and skill will have to accomplish that which one is not motivated to do, or it can mean the difference between focus (the motivators aligned and not closely scored) and balance (the motivators less aligned and the scoring narrowing or close) and which is relevant in a given situation.

3   Motivational Maps describe, measure and monitor motivation. They make our invisible emotional drives visible and quantifiable. At last individuals, managers and organisations can get a handle on this key issue and through Reward Strategies do something about it – namely, increase it. Maps are a complete language and metric of motivation.

4   Motivators change over time. This happens because our beliefs change over time and these belief changes affect how we feel and therefore what motivates us. Thus, regularly monitoring of motivation is appropriate and effective. From a coaching perspective this is so powerful because it is a focused opportunity to explore, too, what one's beliefs are, and whether they are supportive of what one is trying to achieve.

5   Motivational Maps are not a psychometric instrument. Psychometric type tools inevitably describe a 'fixed' personality, a core which is unchanging. Maps are stable but fluid over time. Maps take an 'energy snapshot', for motivation is energy. Technically, Motivational Maps are a Self-Perception Inventory.

6   Motivational Maps do not and cannot stereotype individuals. This follows from the fact they change over time, so whatever someone's profile today, there is no guarantee it will be the same tomorrow. That said, the Maps are usually stable for about 18–24 months. But nobody should suggest, in a personality sort-of-way (e.g. 'I'm an extrovert'), 'I'm a Searcher' or any other motivator.

7   There are nine motivators but they are correlated into three groups. These three groups represent, amongst other things, the three primary modes of human perception: Feeling, Thinking and Knowing. Each perception has fascinating and differing properties.

8   Motivation is highly correlated with performance. It is possible to be a high performer and yet de-motivated, but the price for this, middle or long-term, is stress and health problems. Having a highly motivated workforce is going to reduce illness and absenteeism, as well as presenteeism (the being there in body but not in mind or spirit).

9   Motivation is a feature and people buy benefits. Let's not forget that because motivation is a feature, then it features in many core organisational (and non-organisational) activities: leadership, teams, performance, productivity, sales, appraisal, engagement (70% of engagement is motivation), recruitment, careers and more beside. People, usually therefore, buy the effect or benefit of motivation rather than wanting it directly. Think essential oils! Usually applying an essential oil to the skin requires a 'carrier' oil, so with motivation: it's wrapping the mapping.

What, then, are the nine motivators and what do they mean? The motivators are in an ordered sequence which correlates with Maslow's Hierarchy of Needs. At the base are what we call the Relationship Motivators (R) – representing the desire for security (the Defender), belonging (the Friend), and recognition (the Star). They are represented by the colour green, and they are Relationship Motivators because the primary concern of all three is people orientation.

Then, in sequence we have the three Achievement (A) motivators. These are in the middle of the hierarchy. First, there is the desire for control (the Director), then the desire for money (the Builder), and finally the desire for expertise (the Expert). They are represented by the colour red, and they are Achievement motivators because the primary concern of all three is work orientation.

Finally, we have the three Growth (G) motivators. There are at the top of the hierarchy. These are the desire for innovation (the Creator), then the desire for autonomy (the Spirit), and at the apex – though this does not imply superiority – we have the desire for meaning or purpose (the Searcher). They are represented by the colour blue, and they are Growth motivators because the primary concern of all three is self-orientation.

Figure S.1 The nine Motivators

From this brief re-cap of what Motivational Maps is about we hope that – if you haven't yet encountered them directly – your first response will be: 'That's fascinating – so what is my profile? What are my top three motivators?' A good idea at this point is to request to do a Motivational Map – see endnote 21 of the Preface to find out how to access a Map.

Chapter 1

Unpacking the '4+1' leadership model of leadership

We talked in the Introduction about the four theories of leadership, and how what we wanted was something practical, useful, relevant; and also, something that was 'teachable'. By this we mean that if we take the view that leaders are born, not made, then the whole idea of individuals raising the level of their performance, of stepping up to the mark, is nonsense, since if they weren't born leaders, then nothing is going to make them one. All we can hope for, through our recruitment processes, is that we can find those born to lead us! But of course we do not accept that premise: leaders are made in the furnace of experience (and sometimes affliction) and in the crucible of learning, whether that learning is formally constructed, or informally acquired. In the latter case, such acquisition might well be through what might be called mentoring, or working with a strong role model that one wishes to emulate. Indeed, the learning can occur through a process of 'reverse mentoring': we experience dreadful leadership, note what it's components are, and ever after swear never to do that. Perhaps the best example of this is in parenting – a very important form of leadership: we surely all have met excellent parents who when asked the secret of their success reply that their own parents were so awful they were determined never to bring their own children up like that. So they lead – *parent* – like real parents. The metaphor of the good leader being like a good parent is not that far-fetched either. Many organisations, even today, have positive paternalistic (as well as maternalistic, here especially in some public sector type organisations) cultures where leaders can successfully be surrogate parents to the employees; though this is becoming rarer, as pressure to deliver KPIs[1] accelerates across all types of organisations, and there is less and less time to 'care' – as one would for a loved child – for the staff in a personal way.

Thinking about leadership metaphorically is actually a very powerful way of establishing what leadership is like and just as importantly what it is leadership does. Leaders are *like* parents we are saying. But how are they like parents?

Activity 1.1

Make two lists. In the first, itemise how (good) leadership and (good) parenting are similar. For example, we have already alluded to the fact that both *care* about their charges. How else are they similar? And keep in mind, all metaphors – comparisons – break down at some point. So, how are parents and leaders dissimilar?

There are many points of similarity between good parents and leaders: caring, commitment, honesty, reliability, vision for their future, investment in their learning and development, which is also teaching and training, interdependence, results, pride, and ultimately autonomy. And many more similarities too. But there are also dissimilarities: leaders may need to subordinate all personal issues in order to achieve the organisational mission, but for parents the child is the mission; leaders are not usually related by blood to employees, whereas for family this is usually critical; leaders tend to be more aware, more objective about the values underpinning their actions, whereas parents tend to be more subjective and more accepting, so less critical, of what their values are. We could go on, but we hope the point is clear: metaphors provide instructive and directive images as to what something – in this case, leadership – means in a given context. But leadership as parenting is just one metaphor.

Activity 1.2

Think about another metaphor for leadership. What is leadership *like*?

Leadership is …

Note and explain why, in your example, the metaphor and leadership are similar.

It may seem strange, this working in metaphors, but in fact it is the essence not of childishness, but of maturity, and it is fundamental to our appreciation of the world because it enables us to see the invisible relationship between things, ideas and processes. Metaphor is essentially dynamic – precisely what leadership is. If we wish to capture the essence of the dynamism of leadership we will use a metaphor in order to 'grasp' it; if we wish to compartmentalise leadership and exhibit essentially static models we will use competency boxes. Both models have their uses, but the former is far more inspiring, and far more likely to motivate than the latter. And once we can do that, then we may be able to break the metaphor down into helpful parts.

Here is, then, what we see as a brilliant metaphor for leadership: leadership as/is a performing art.[2] Peter Vaill considers three main ways (or subsidiary metaphors) in which leadership is theatre. See Figure 1.1.

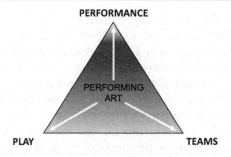

Figure 1.1 Leadership as a performing art

Leadership is a performance

There is an 'up-front-ness' about leadership, which is undeniable even in the most retiring leaders. The performance we must remember is essentially task-orientated: the purpose is to do the performance, and before an audience. Thus, a good leader must be outcome orientated, since audiences are always evaluating what we do. The essence of any stage performance, of course, is motivation: whether the leader is the star on stage, or the director of the play, motivation leads and drives what they are doing.

Leadership is intrinsically connected to teamwork

Yes, the star on stage may well be the leader, but the play – the performance – can only be as good as the weakest member of the cast. Unless rehearsals involve everybody, performance – no matter how 'strong' the leader – will be weak. A strong personality who does not pay attention to his staff proves a weak leader, and clearly is exercising 'personality' at everyone else's expense. But again, since even the weakest link is vital in a stage performance to make the whole presentation 'authentic' or 'compelling', then the leader has to, or find means to, motivate everyone. Team motivation, like individual motivation, is vital.

Leadership is about 'play'

Theatre is a play in both senses of the word. There is a recreation and re-creation in the activity. It is what we all complain we have lost. As children our 'work' was our 'play', and thoroughly enjoyable it was too! We didn't want anyone to send us to bed. Now, we find we collapse only too readily in bed, exhausted by work – a work that is devoid of 'play'. This is a vital thing about our leadership activity we need to re-discover: that work should and must be a form of play, or that play is somehow integral to it, and if it is not then we are heading for trouble. Overtime – overwork – has no psychological meaning when we 'play' (are being creative), since the only limits are those that the task itself defines for us, and which we readily accept. But we are invariably motivated to play; why is that? Because play meets our motivators head-on. When we are really playing, that is, not doing the play prescribed for us by others, we are intrinsically interested in what we are doing and so time stops. We stop counting the clock and become absorbed. We enter the zone, or what Mihaly Csikszentmihalyi called the 'flow'[3] state. These metaphors, then, all lead us back to a fundamental fact that we cannot help repeating: the centrality of motivation at the heart of leadership; for motivation, too, flows. Which means, also, that it is dynamic.

Thus, to get a sense of what leadership is – a performing art – and one driven by motivation is to begin to get a sense of its true nature. This nature involves flow; it involves responding to reality in the moment; but it also involves a clear picture of what the final 'work' looks like. And so another word we can introduce here is change: good leaders, great leaders are individuals who master change, who make it happen in order to deliver a better outcome for an organisation or entity than would otherwise be the case.[4] To do this they are architects (a metaphor!) of the strategy which it is necessary to devise and put in place. But in short, to put it at its most dramatic: leadership is about life, because change is life; for if we cannot cross the bridge and get from A to B, if we remain stuck at A – and there is no change – we die, either literally or metaphorically. Take a moment to think about this practically: in the UK (and USA and everywhere else) long-established companies and organisations are dying – going bust and closing down – because they had not been led to respond to the changes. Perhaps the most famous example of this is the rise of the internet,[5] and Amazon specifically, as a retail force. Its attack on the shopping habits of customers in the high streets and malls has been nothing short of amazing. Major stores in the UK such as British Home Stores, Maplins, Toys "R" Us, HMV have all gone to the wall. But other stores, for example, Next, Aldi and Waitrose, have continued to thrive despite the online onslaught. Why is this? At the end of the day it will almost certainly be down to the leadership, and specifically the leader; for leaders are those who are awake – they see the writing on the wall and take action to avert it. Even better, the truly great leaders see the writing on the wall and interpret it not as a threat, but an opportunity to be embraced. So, they and their organisations emerge stronger from the threat.

As it happens, then, our model of the '4+1', whilst neatly compartmentalised in a way metaphors are not, captures the essence of what needs to happen to develop leaders, so that they become a living 'performing art', and perform, build teams, play and more beside. This essence starts with the individual and their empowerment and developing capabilities, and leads on to the teams and organisations and their realisation of their full potential. Great leaders become the best they can be, and they enable those they lead to do the same. Notice that in saying this there is a strong moral and ethical dimensions to leadership.[6]

So our model looks like Figure 1.2.

Figure 1.2 Motivational Maps '4+1' model of leadership

Before we start unpacking this model in depth (and see Figure 4.1 for a short diagnostic of using this) in Chapter 2, let's consider all the five ('4+1'!) elements of it in turn to get a sense of what we are talking about and how Motivational Maps is relevant to it.

First, and most critically of all, true leadership begins with the Self. What is the Self? The Self is the modern psychological term used to describe what in the past we called the soul. What this Self or soul is lies beyond the scope of this book, but one does not need to be specifically religious to resonate with the idea, common all over the world, "that there is some part of us which should not be sold, betrayed or lost at any cost".[7] It is who we are at a root level; and one only needs to reflect that everybody – yes, everybody – at some point in their life talks to themselves; indeed, many people do it all the time. But who are we speaking to when we talk to ourselves? It is as if there are two people present in this self-dialogue. The intellect or the mind or the ego, perhaps talking to the deeper Self, the soul, and if it waits long enough, getting answers back.[8]

The important point to realise here and stress is that the Self is not the ego: it is not, therefore, our rational, conscious minds, although our awareness of it – through say its dialoguing with our ego – can be very conscious. It may manifest itself also through intuition, instinct and conscience. But, what our ego is driving us to do is not necessarily what our Self wants us to do. There can be a disconnect, which is why, and how, we can become inauthentic: not truly ourselves! This is why, too, it's no good just the ego deciding to get 'trained up' to be a great leader. Training per se can lead to a superficial acquisition of skills and knowledge but the deeper part of us still lacks commitment, understanding and belief. A key word here might be that we are not integrous, or whole: if the ego is not aligned with the Self, there will be serious problems.

Activity 1.3

Given our description of the ego and the Self, what kind of serious problems do you envisage might emerge if there is no congruence between them? What are the three most important, or serious issues from the perspective of leadership and being a leader?

From the point of view of leadership, we think there are at least three mission-fatal outcomes:

Leaders fail to walk the talk –

employees perceive personal and organisational inconsistency, lack of fairness, selfishness

Leaders fail to be open or to embrace ambiguity –

employees perceive a rigid, prescriptive, 'right' approach, which the ego always prefers

Leaders fail to innovate –

employees perceive a lack of flexibility, a single-minded focus on profit, and a complacency based on successes now, rather than in future, which leads to chronic short-termism.

There are of course other adverse outcomes too, but these three, any one of which, are fatal to success since they all undermine belief and confidence in leadership, commitment and engagement to the role and mission, and the ability to create an attractive future. With these serious and deleterious effects in mind, then, it behoves us to take the development of the Self as a matter of primary importance. The beginning of this process has to be increasing self-awareness. This is foundational – we can only grow as individuals, and as leaders, if we are self-aware, truly self-aware. And this self-awareness includes physical, mental, emotional and spiritual dimensions.

Furthermore, to become self-aware we need a range of options to enable this to happen. Self-reflection is a good start, and accepting feedback from others is huge advantage. But we see in Figure 1.3 some other important elements of this: we have to commit to self-development if we are to attain personal 'growth'. If we cannot commit, then we cannot grow. If we consider all this some sort of namby-pamby, hippy, new age gobbledygook, then obviously commitment will be lacking. But given that commitment, we can seriously approach developing our own self-awareness; here Motivational Maps is one vital tool. Two others are: considering the Self in its four manifestations of physical, mental, emotional and spiritual; and probing our own self-concept,[9] and its three component parts.

Figure 1.3 Motivational leadership and the Self

One of the curious paradoxes of true and deep learning, and of the real experts who truly have become 'gurus' in their field, is their almost universal testimony to the fact that the greater the expertise they have, the greater their awareness is of all that they don't know. Their self-awareness of what they know contrasts ever more vividly with the scale of what they don't know, and this itself has a personal growth effect in that it seems to engender humility and a real willingness and desire (motivation) to learn even more. Contrast this with the 'know-it-all', the person with a tiny bit of knowledge in a tiny field, who remains stuck in the rut of their extremely limited competence.[10]

Activity 1.4

How important is self-awareness to you? Would you describe yourself as 'self-aware'? If yes, what proof do you have that is so? If not, then why not? What has prevented you from being self-aware? What could you do to increase your self-awareness? Do you have a process for developing self-awareness? What tools might help you increase your self-awareness?

Five cost-effective ways[11] to improve your self-awareness are:

1   acquiring quality feedback;
2   using diagnostic profiling tools;
3   starting a journal;
4   challenging yourself to leave your 'comfort zone';
5   imagining ... what if ...?

Activity 1.5

Do not attempt to become more self-aware by undertaking all five ways simultaneously! Instead choose one way that appeals to you and make a plan to work it for at least six months, and track your progress.

1   Where and who will you get good quality feedback from? Consider the feedback that might help you in the following areas: your qualities, your performance/capabilities, and your situation. List the people you know, like and trust – who can help? When and how will you ask them? What organisations can help you? How can you access them and their expertise? From a strictly leadership point of view acquiring a coach or mentor can turbo-charge your performance precisely because of the quality of feedback that they can provide.

2   What diagnostic profiles will you complete? Motivational Maps is one tool; what about personality tests or psychometric assessments? Consider strengths and weakness inventories, or team or learning styles diagnostics like Belbin[12] and Kolb.[13] What will you do with them when they are done? One thing might be to ask somebody who knows you well to comment on the accuracy of the profiles(s). Another key task is to compare the type of person you are with the type of work you do – is there a fit?

3   Review your own life in detail: what you have done speaks volumes about the real 'you', not the imaginary 'you', or the false 'you' that you have inadvertently constructed over time in your own mind. When will you start your own journal? Log at least three achievements per day. Review your week and month regularly, spot patterns. What have you achieved over the last three days specifically? Remember, this is a key issue in building self-esteem; it builds a portfolio of evidence that becomes believable even to the subconscious mind – yours!

4   Challenge yourself to leave your comfort zone. What activity will you undertake? Usually new learning is necessary to do something never done before. What would make you proud if you did it? What did you want to do as a child or young person, but never did? What would give you a real stretch? Remember, if all this seems difficult, that children do this all the time: they sing in public for the first time, they undertake complex work, they go on some adventure trek – and as a result they grow at a tremendous rate. They drive themselves to their limits. One word of caution: going out of the comfort zone is not to be confused with doing bizarre and dangerous things just because they are there, or because others do them.

5   Imagining …or daydreaming and asking 'what if?' When will you visualise? How? And under what conditions? Stay relaxed. Make notes… visualise yourself with knowledge, skills, talents that appeal to you. By focusing your mind on what you want or even on finding what you want, a powerful force is unleashed. The power of the imagination is virtually unlimited; everything that is came into existence via the imagination: it was seen in the mind's eye before it was 'created' literally or physically. Thus the more time is spent imaging ideal 'realities', the more likely it is that reality will come to pass. It is important that when using visualisation and imaging techniques that you stay in a relaxed state of mind.

Which one of the five have you chosen to work on over the next six months?

These five techniques will certainly boost self-awareness, and understanding of one's strengths and weaknesses; they are, therefore, indispensable (in their selective way) to the whole idea of developing effective leadership.

We have begun, then, a first take on becoming more self-aware and in subsequent chapters we shall take this further. But let us now consider the first skill of the '4': Thinking. George S Patton, the famous military general of World War Two famously said: "If everybody is thinking alike then somebody isn't thinking".[14] This doesn't tell us what 'thinking' is, but it points towards our knowing when it isn't happening: when everybody agrees! So from a leadership perspective three issues should be clear: one, that leaders themselves are often going to be people who take a different viewpoint to the consensus opinion; two, that leaders tolerate and even encourage diverse opinions and innovative solutions; and three, that thinking is hard because it necessarily entails divergence and potential conflict. It's much easier to conform, to go with the herd, and keep one's head down and not rock the boat. From a motivational viewpoint this conformity is correlated much more acutely with the Defender-type motivator, because the need for security will by necessity be wary of change, and of the 'new thinking' that threatens to upset the apple cart or the status quo. This does not mean, of course, that individuals who have Defender as their number 1 motivator are unfit to be leaders; absolutely not. But it does mean that such individuals need to be self-aware, extremely self-aware, of their propensity to play it safe – and where appropriate to compensate[15] for it.

Activity 1.6

'Thinking' seems such a simple thing to do,[16] so consider: what do leaders need to think about when they lead an organisation? List four or five key areas and prioritise.

Leaders are different because they think; and in the case of leading an organisation they think about its past, its present and most importantly of all, about its future. What kind of future will it have, and how are they are going to transition it from A to B? In other words, the strategy they will deploy.

We think leadership thinking has four core components: the big picture, which comprises the what we can be, what we do, and what we believe in. Two words missing from this Figure 1.4 but underpinning vision, mission and values are the words culture and engagement. It's all very well having a brilliant vision, being clear about what we do,[17] and having strong values underpinning the organisation's activities, BUT these will never be realised unless employees are engaged and the whole culture is positive, supportive and pro-active. Which means that the thinking about stage b, the strategizing, planning and goal setting has to be largely exploratory – how we get there

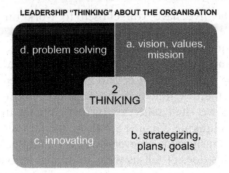

Figure 1.4 Leadership thinking about the organisation

and get there through people, since it is people who realise the culture and operate as engaged or otherwise. When this is truly working, then the employees will be innovative and they will problem solve. But keep in mind, the thinking from the leader's point of view may begin in reverse: they have just been appointed to an organisation with little vision, insincere values and no real mission, and no strategy or plan except to continue doing what they have always done, and so no innovation in product or people development, or marketing and sales, is occurring; so the starting point is to problem solve that very issue by considering very carefully HOW? And, it should come as no surprise, if one were faced with just such a situation that a good, counter-intuitive starting point would be the motivation of all employees. It is unlocking the energy within the staff that should be of paramount importance if we are truly 'thinking' about how to get from A to B. After all, we are talking about a long journey: knowing the right direction is essential, having the right equipment is necessary, but not to consider the fitness, commitment and energy levels of the travellers is insane. Thus, when we come to consider leadership thinking, we shall put Motivational Maps at the heart of the process, as we do in Chapter 4.

Next, we come to a brief overview of the 'Doing' skill. What do leaders 'do'?

Activity 1.7

In your opinion, what are the three or four most important things that leader do? Jot down your best ideas and when you have, put them in a rank order, if you can.

First, leaders need to take control of their time, which means effectively prioritising what is and isn't important,[18] and this also means handling meetings and allowing projects to run smoothly; for both meetings and projects are forms of time management in that if they are not handled well, they lead to enormous wastes of time and effort, and so are absolutely demoralising, demotivating, disengaging when done consistently poorly. Indeed, 'meetings' are often cited as the first or second biggest waste of time in organisational life;[19] nearly everyone seems to hate them or at best to regard them as the main distraction from getting on with 'real' work. So, the leader must deal with this because – when you think about it – how can there not be meetings if we need to produce team focus and alignment in our targeted activities?

Second, it is said of Human Resources (HR) that they have three functions, the 3 Rs: to Recruit staff, to Retain staff (the best and the good!), and to Remove staff (the worst and the superfluous). Essentially, though, this is what the leader has to ensure is happening; it is sometimes said that recruiting is itself the number 1 skill of any leader, as failure to do it well has such dreadful ramifications for the organisation in the short and long term. Furthermore, recruitment now has become far more complex than it once was: issues of equality, diversity and more, have made this not only an organisational issue, but a political one. Leaders have to steer an acceptable course in order not only to select the most effective employees, but also to present a positive face to the wider community in which they operate. Motivational Maps is by its nature a non-stereotyping diagnostic, as we will see, and so can provide valuable insights for the leader in this task: Chapter 7 specifically addresses the issue of how Motivational Maps can help remove leaders who underperform or are simply in at a level beyond their competence.

But having got the best people in, we need to retain them. At the highest levels of performance, people work for its own sake: their intrinsic motivation in what they are doing; at the lesser levels they work for rewards. But at both levels there are rewards: intrinsic and extrinsic. Understanding how these work psychologically, and having a system, particularly one locked into the appraisal system, that is geared round rewards is vital. Here Motivational Maps can make a major contribution and we look at this in Chapter 5.

The last two boxes of Figure 1.5 – implementing and turn-key operations – have less to do with motivation per se, so we will cover these only in passing,

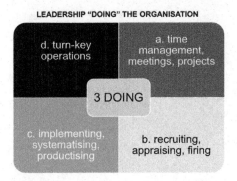

Figure 1.5 Leadership 'doing' the organisation

but they are certainly aspirational in nature: a turn-key operation is really creating a business that can function even when we do not! For some leaders this is psychologically difficult, for they need to be needed, or they need to be at the centre of all the activities. So turn-key operations that require minimal input can be extremely challenging. Are leaders going to be busy – as in busy-busy – or are they going to be effective?

These first two skills – Thinking and Doing – we note in Figure 1.2 are working "On the Organisation". In other words, they focus on what the organisation itself is going to become. But the second two skills – Team Building and Motivating – we describe as working "In the Organisation", because their focus is internal, and this is so in recognition of the vital importance of enabling, empowering and engaging employees to deliver on the Thinking and Doing. In our experience, and we think it typical, we would claim there is too much done 'on the organisation' and not enough 'in the organisation'; hence the massive wastage of people within organisations and the consistently low figures for actual staff engagement.[20]

So, our third skill is Team Building. In a way this is special kind of 'Doing', but so important that it requires a chapter of its own. All great leaders form powerful, effective and empowered teams that – unleashed – go out and do great things on behalf of the organisation.

Activity 1.8

Why are teams so important to organisations and organisational life? What, in your view, constitutes a real team? What qualities do they share and exhibit?

There is possibly almost as much research on team building and teams as there is on leadership;[21] it is a phenomenally popular subject, and not surprisingly: there is the basic, and correct, perception that 'Together Each Achieves More' (T.E.A.M). What this means is that teamwork is not an arithmetical process whereby having five people in a team means we get five

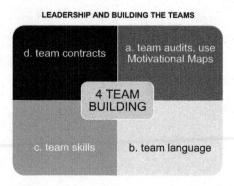

Figure 1.6 Leadership and building the teams

units of work – no, that would simply be a group of people. A key distinction (are we a team or are we a group?) we like to make. Teams provide a geometric power – like with money and compound interest – over time small sums, small teams, can produce extraordinary amounts of cash, energy and outcomes.

The powers of the leader include enlisting others (recruitment and deployment), enabling others to act (empowerment), strengthening others (encouragement, inspiration, training and development) and fostering collaboration (the true test of a team). And here, as we shall see Motivational Maps can play a crucial role; perhaps more crucial than in any other application of Maps. Which means, this is absolutely essential for leaders to understand and use.

The key thing to grasp here is that motivation is about employees' energy; and teams without energy are dead teams. Maps can audit that energy, see where it is strong and where it is weak, and see where different team members have conflicting energies and subconscious desires, and see where the motivational profile either helps or hinders the objectives that the team is trying to achieve. In the first instance, after the team motivational audit, the Maps provide a neutral language in which each individual's contribution can be discussed without judgement. Reward strategies can be put in place to increase energy and motivation. From that position, team skills can be reviewed and a team contract drawn up that enables the staff to work far more smoothly and effectively than they otherwise would. We shall be looking at this in far more detail, and how to do it, in Chapter 6.

Finally, leaders have a personal responsibility to motivate their employees. Specifically, their immediate reports – their personal team, as it were – but, depending on their seniority, all those below them in the hierarchy. So, if they are the CEO, then they are responsible for the motivation of all staff; the buck stops with them. Everything they do will contribute to adding to the motivation of the organisation, or of diminishing it. In some ways it could be argued that this is the most difficult and demanding area of leadership, for it

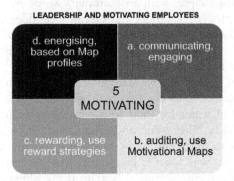

Figure 1.7 Leadership and motivating employees

can almost seem a waste of valuable time! Big organisations with big visions and big objectives, sure, thinking, doing and team building make sense. Even developing one's self-awareness and capabilities have a logic; but why spend time motivating people who are already being well paid to get on with their jobs? It can seem a distraction. But as Marcus Aurelius, the Roman emperor and philosopher, observed:[22] "The secret of all victory lies in the organisation of the non-obvious", and here is a classic case of the non-obvious. But Maps provide the ultimate way of obtaining some serious traction on this non-obvious facet of organisational life.

In general terms motivating employees involves what we call in an earlier book[23] 'interpersonal skills'. These interpersonal skills enable us to communicate clearly and engage staff. They involve empathy, appreciation and non-verbal communication, listening and decision making skills, as well as the capacity to negotiate, as opposed to command all the time. But all these skills are massively enhanced and multiplied if the use of them is targeted by actually knowing what motivates each individual with whom one comes into contact; especially, regular contact.

So again, we need to do a Motivational Map audit and start practising deploying reward strategies that genuinely do motivate employees. Only in this way can we truly energise our staff to their maximum effect. As we say, Motivational Maps describe the motivators, measure and monitor them, and finally enable us to maximise them. In Chapter 8 we study this in much more depth.

It should be clear in this overview of the leadership '4+1' model how intrinsic and vital to leadership motivation is. As we said in the Introduction, some 50% or more of leadership comes down to some aspect of motivation. Without motivation, without energy, not only is the leader powerless, but is attempting to lead those who, like the Lotus Eaters on the mythical island that Odysseus[24] reached, simply cannot be led, for they have no energy – their situation is hopeless, for they can never escape from where they are: change is impossible.

Let's conclude this chapter with an exemplary story, not from Greek myth, but from Greek history: Alexander the Great. One does not approve of his violence and bloodshed, but as a leader he was nothing short of phenomenal in several categories, not least of which was motivating his men. Alexander, having disastrously led his men into the Bactrian desert,[25] and facing a calamitous shortage of water which threatened to destroy his army, which no other army had been able to do, two men who had gone ahead came back carrying two skins of water for their sons who were suffering in the column. Meeting the king, they filled a cup and offered him the water. Keep in mind, all were parched with thirst and many had already died. Alexander took the cup and asked who it was for. On learning it was for their sons, he returned the cup untouched, saying, "I cannot bear to drink alone and it is not possible for me to share so little with everybody. Go quickly and give your sons what you have brought on their account". Clearly, Alexander did not use a Motivational Map in this instance, but he understood something with total clarity: how important each individual in his whole army was, and that as king it was not for him to lord it over them, but to share in their sufferings. Leaders need to lead and in such actions we see the quintessence of true leadership; indeed, of true greatness.

We are almost certainly not going to be in an Alexander the Great situation in our own positions of leadership, but when we come down to it we are going to need those inner resources that Alexander abundantly had. And so the beginning, as we move into Chapter 2, is certainly personal development.

Notes

1 KPI – Key Performance Indicator: "Key performance indicators (KPI) are a set of quantifiable measures that a company uses to gauge its performance over time. These metrics are used to determine a company's progress in achieving its strategic and operational goals, and also to compare a company's finances and performance against other businesses within its industry" – see https://bit.ly/2HHk3gI.
2 Peter B Vaill, *Managing as a Performing Art*, Jossey-Bass (1989).
3 Mihaly Csikszentmihalyi, *Flow*, Rider; New Ed edition (2002).
4 "A leader's responsibility then is to help develop conceptual designs for changes at the process level" – G J Langley, K M Nolan, T W Nolan, C L Norman and L P Provost, *The Improvement Guide*, Jossey-Bass (1996).
5 "E-commerce accounted for a 19 percent share of total business turnover in the United Kingdom in 2015. As of 2015, roughly 80 percent of UK internet users did online shopping, the highest online shopping penetration rate in Europe" – https://bit.ly/2vINnib.
6 Vision that is not centred in profound spirituality is nothing more than a "pictorial might-be of an organisation's future ... what metaphors and images are real for me as I move into spiritual leadership? ... All true leadership is indeed spiritual leadership ... the reason is... leadership is concerned with bringing out the best in people... as such one's best is tied intimately to one's deepest sense of oneself, to one's spirit. My leadership efforts must touch that in myself and in others" – Peter B Vaill, ibid.
7 Patrick Harpur, *A Complete Guide to the Soul*, Rider: Ebury Publishing (2010).
8 See James Sale and Bevis Moynan, *Mapping Motivation for Coaching*, Routledge (2018) for more on this.
9 For more on the self-concept and its three components see, James Sale, *Mapping Motivation*, Routledge (2016), Chapter 2.
10 See James Sale, *Mapping Motivation*, ibid.
11 I am indebted to Dave Francis' *Managing Your Own Career*, Collins (1985) for these ideas.
12 For more on Belbin team roles go to: https://bit.ly/1FjH07x.
13 For more on Kolb's theory go to: https://bit.ly/2LP3Ok1.
14 https://bit.ly/2tuydwr – George S Patton.
15 For example, often a great practical way a highly cautious leader offsets their natural tendency is by appointing an opposite type as their number two. This applies of course in reverse: a too-risk friendly leader (that is to say one with a strong set

of Growth motivators in their top three) may well have a much more conservative number 2 to restrain their over-enthusiastic embrace of new ideas.

16 Though as Thomas Edison observed, caustically: "Five percent of the people think; ten percent of the people think they think; and the other eighty-five percent would rather die than think" – https://bit.ly/2MdYmqX.

17 Peter Drucker put this succinctly when he said, "Culture eats strategy for lunch" – https://bit.ly/2G470Zj. This expression seems to derive from Edgar Schein: "More and more management consultants are recognizing these types of problems and are noting explicitly that, because 'culture constrains strategy,' a company must analyze its culture and learn to manage within its boundaries or, if necessary, change it" *Organizational Culture and Leadership* (1985).

18 And as we know from Stephen Covey's work, what is important and what is urgent are not the same thing. *First Things First*, with A Roger Merrill, Prentice Hall (1995).

19 For example, see https://bit.ly/2lzbBY8.

20 See, James Sale and Steve Jones, *Mapping Motivation for Engagement*, Routledge (2018), Introductory chapter.

21 On the day of writing this, a search in Amazon.co.uk for 'leadership' produced 60,000+ books, whereas a search for 'teams' produced 50,000+. Close!

22 For more on this quotation see: https://bit.ly/2Kmdbuj.

23 James Sale and Steve Jones, *Mapping Motivation for Engagement*, ibid.

24 *The Odyssey*, Homer, translated Robert Fitzgerald, Vintage Classics (2007).

25 See https://bit.ly/2lBldS7.

Chapter 2

Developing your Self (the '+1') as leader

We now arrive at the point of considering the primary element of leadership, what we are calling the '+1' in our formula: personal development, personal growth and all underpinned by a commitment to expanding our own self-awareness. Before we introduce more on Motivational Maps, let's consider some more generic approaches to developing our self-awareness. Keep in mind at all times that progression is not likely to be linear; that sometimes we take three steps forward, but also end up making two steps back. Developing new habits and practices takes time; and furthermore, leadership is not simply about cognitive ability. To say this means at least two things: one, the brightest person in the room is not necessarily going to make the best leader; and two, that whilst we encourage education[1] and learning, it is not the accumulation of passed examinations and letters behind one's name that proves one is 'qualified' to lead. As we go on repeating: leadership is ambiguous and, like people, sometimes mysterious too.

Perhaps, then, a starting point might be to review oneself how to be a better leader, and to do this by simply trying to access one's deeper subconscious wisdom. One way of approaching this is by using what has been called Mindstorming[2] or the 20-Question Method. The basic idea is to formulate a SMART – specific, measurable, achievable, relevant and time-trackable question which stimulates the imagination. Such questions need to be tailored to the domain in which we are operating; so, for example, in sales it might be:

"How can I increase sales over the next three months?"

Or, in interpersonal relationships it might be:

"How can I improve the relationship between Chris and John next week?"

Clearly, any area of organisational life could benefit from the scrutiny of a correctly phrased question. Having formulated the question in this way, the next step is to write down 20 answers to it! Yes, that's right: 20 answers. It doesn't matter if the answers contradict each (e.g. invest money in training *versus* cut the training budget), so long as you generate the 20 answers, and do so within a restricted time frame – say, 30 or 60 minutes.

Activity 2.1

How can I be a more effective leader over the next six-month period?

Usually, the first few answers (see Figure 2.1) are easy, but it gets increasingly difficult to generate them. However, the act of 'forcing' answers from the conscious, and increasingly subconscious, mind can lead to breathtaking insights and solutions. Also, remember that whatever your role or job, everyone is a leader to someone else at some point in their lives;[3] and this includes home life too.

In reviewing your answers, what do you learn about yourself? Which of your self-suggestions seem most relevant and powerful? Is there a pattern in what they are? Are they tangible, intangible or people development issues? Or a little of each?Tangible: about money, equipment, or space/environment?

How can I be a more effective leader over the next 6 months?
1
2
3
4
5
6
7
8
9
10
11
12
13
14
15
16
17
18
19
20

Figure 2.1 20 Answers to being a more effective leader

Intangible: about time, knowledge, or information?

People development: about people skills, right attitude, or agreed co-operation?

There is no right and wrong here, but what do you need to do to be a better leader?

This, then, is a starter. But even more seriously we now need to begin the raising of that self-awareness that is critical for the necessary personal development which is the journey – the arc – of the true leader. And this raising of self-awareness can be done in a number of ways,[4] but we think that so far as leadership is concerned there are two critical methodologies: namely,

1   acquiring quality feedback
2   using diagnostic profiling tools.

Americans have this wonderful expression that 'feedback is the breakfast of champions'; it's all about winning, about becoming the best you that you can possibly be. And the truth is that without feedback we are doomed to drift: we simply cannot see enough of ourselves, clearly enough, accurately enough, powerfully enough, to be able through our own resources to steer successfully across the stormy ocean of life, be it organisational life or personal. This is especially true of what Jung called our 'shadow' self, the part of us that often we don't want to see as it disturbs our comfortable self-image.[5] Put more directly, how do we see our own back and the backs of own heads? We need instruments, like mirrors, that is to say a diagnostic, and we need someone else to tell us what is behind us! We are reminded of that famous UK TV 'Fast Show' sketch[6] from the 1990s where one woman's catchphrase was 'Does my bum look big in this?' Even with a mirror she couldn't tell herself!

So, we all need feedback and we all crave it. Sometimes we don't call it feedback, but something else; for as William James observed,[7] 'The deepest principle in human nature is the craving to be appreciated.' But it is all aspects of the same thing: feedback, recognition, appreciation, even 'soul food', for that is what quality feedback is. We like to use the phrase 'quality feedback', although it may be called other things, such as 'constructive' feedback. Clearly, though, some feedback can be outright nasty, unhelpful and demeaning. What we are looking for is the kind of feedback that encourages, develops and 'grows' people,[8] especially leaders.

Our first methodology is acquiring quality feedback. But where do we get quality feedback from?

Looking at Figure 2.2 we see that there are three sources of quality feedback and three questions to further address the issue. So far as teams and the organisation go, the feedback we need tends to be not personal so much as statistical and outcome orientated. But it is in the area of personal feedback that the most important opportunities for personal growth occur. We need to keep in mind one essential principle: namely, that it is vital to solicit quality feedback from positive and constructive people. All leaders, more or less, have

Where do I currently get quality feedback from?

INDIVIDUALS	TEAMS	ORGANISATION
	Productivity	Customers
	Targets	Suppliers
	Engagement	Reputation
		Market share

MOTIVATION $\longrightarrow$

Where could I get quality feedback from?

INDIVIDUALS	TEAMS	ORGANISATION

What will I do to get quality feedback for the ensuing year?

INDIVIDUALS	TEAMS	ORGANISATION

Figure 2.2 Acquiring quality feedback as a leader

to put up with carping criticism or destructive, self-interested attacks masquerading as 'positive' feedback, but which are anything but. But it is only from individual's who genuinely care about us or the mission from whom we can really derive sustenance. Hence these 3 questions.

Activity 2.2

Take time to review these 3 questions (as in Figure 2.2 and below) carefully as a leader. Think about the kind of person whom you really think can help you grow. Think, too, more widely than internal employees or staff you have, though their feedback may be valuable. Think about external peers at your level, about possible mentors who operate at a higher level than you, and think about consultants and coaches who may be able to give you an additional edge in your work. Where *could* you get more and better feedback from? Where do you currently get quality feedback from? Where could you get quality feedback from? What will you do to get more quality feedback in the ensuing year?

The final question requires you create an action plan based on your review.

These are standard ways of thinking about feedback. Using Motivational Maps, however, can give leaders a big advantage by accelerating their self-awareness, and by providing manageable and doable reward strategies that enable them to increase their motivation, their energy and their resilience to perform. The most obvious way is simply by doing a Map; ideally doing it, and then receiving expert feedback from a qualified Motivational Map practitioner.

Mark was the Operational Director of a significant medium-sized company that provided high tech security hardware to organisations across the world; furthermore, he was a minority equity stakeholder in the company. However, despite his very senior position and holdings within the company, he felt that he was consistently underperforming, that he was being undermined (but not maliciously) by the Managing Director whose expectations were different from his own, and more generally he felt he lacked confidence in himself. But, he was/is a leader, so where to go from there?

Mark, therefore, asked co-author, James, to help him develop as a leader, and to specifically address issues of confidence, engaging with others through effective networking, and achieving goals. And the starting point was his Motivational Map and what that revealed.

Activity 2.3

Consider the 16 numbers[9] on Mark's Map (Figure 2.3[10]). What, if anything, does it tell you? What can you glean from these numbers? More specifically, if

Motivational Map Summary for Mark's first Map			
Motivator	Position	Score	PMA (/10)
Spirit	1	27	3
Defender	2	26	2
Searcher	3	24	5
Expert	4	22	
Builder	5	20	
Creator	6	18	
Star	7	16	
Director	8	15	
Friend	9	12	
PMA Score	29%		
RAG scores:	30:32:38		

Figure 2.3 Mark's Motivational Map – 16 numbers

you look at these numbers what might be useful in raising Mark's levels of self-awareness?

Let's keep in mind that Mark was already to a certain degree self-aware: he knew he had a problem or problems in his leadership role; he had decided that it could not be resolved within the confines of his organisation; he had privately – without his Managing Director knowing about it (since he felt that would provide ammunition to his boss about his 'weaknesses', and as he was already feeling weak, this was the last thing he wanted) commissioned a coach to help him. But what next emerged from the Map shocked even Mark.

The first thing that shocked Mark was his Personal Motivational Score (PMA) score of 29%. Yes, he knew that he was not as motivated as he once was, but to discover that he was in the lowest and Action Zone (or Quadrant, see Figure 2.4) of motivation, and not even borderline (at 35%) with the next level up (the Risk Zone) was truly chilling. Why? Because we made it plain that such a low level of motivation not only impacted his possible performance levels detrimentally, but that if he continued working with those 'low' and sinking energy feelings, then he would almost certainly encounter a health or wellness problem at some time in the near future. As soon as this was pointed out, Mark recognised the truth of the observation, and this became a spur for him to get 'sorted'.

Second, Mark was doubly disturbed to discover that Director (15/40) and Friend (12/40) were his two lowest motivators; the disturbance arose because of the fact that knowing this meant challenging his own self-image – that is, who he saw himself being at some core level of his personality. In the first instance, to be so senior within the company and yet to learn that managing people (the Director motivator) was not really what he wanted to do – but actually what he was required to, and was doing! That was a wake-up call too. Then, even worse, since Mark seemed an extremely friendly and sociable 'bloke' (to use an English colloquialism) to find out that relationships at work were the least important thing for him – when, as we say, he considered himself 'friendly', was a jolt. And because the implications were all too clear to him: he imagined he was managing, but actually was he in reality avoiding the real issues of management by prioritising other activities; and also was he as well-liked as he thought he was? Indeed, was there a backlash of complaints about him to the CEO which was why he felt under such pressure?

Third, and certainly not least, as we came to discuss his top three motivators, the ones that actually were driving him at work, and the ones that he felt

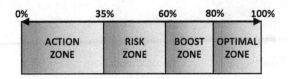

Figure 2.4 The four quadrants of motivation

were being unsatisfied (his Spirit motivator scored only 3/10, his Defender 2/10, and his Searcher 5/10), we discover, especially between his top and second motivator, an internal conflict of a quite severe nature. Consider the scores: his top motivator, Spirit, is 27/40 in terms of importance, and is only 3/10 satisfied. His second motivator, Defender, is 26/40 in terms of importance, and only 2/10 satisfied. What's important to realise here is that they are closely scored; there is only a one-point difference in terms of their importance to Mark (27–26). But – and here is the critical point – they are pulling him in entirely different directions.

The Spirit – Mark wants to be free and autonomous
The Defender – Mark wants to be secure and safe.

However, freedom involves having more risk and so more change; security, on the contrary, involves reducing risk and minimising change. Effectively, Mark is driving his car with the accelerator (Spirit) on at the same time as he is applying the brake (Defender)! Wow, no wonder his performance is muted. And not only performance, but actually clarity too: for what does Mark really want from work? At this point it is important to say that a motivational conflict within one's motivators, especially at the top-3 level, is not necessarily a problem; indeed, contextually, this can be an asset because the nature of the role requires different and conflicting motivators to be deliverable. A good example of this we frequently find is in Accountancy practices, where often (not always) two specific motivators conflict: Searcher (making a difference for the client, and so making changes) and Defender (seeking to be secure and safe). But in the case of accountancy, often the drive to be secure and safe whilst making that difference for the client is via accuracy, procedures, and careful analysis. So in that context the motivators can work well; but this is not the case with Mark.

Here Mark is wanting to be more autonomous, but the working environment is dedicated to processes and systems which inhibit that; and he wants to be personally safe and secure in his role, but cannot be because he cannot do the things that he thinks are right or better for the organisation. So neither motivator gets met. Clearly, resolving this motivational conflict is at the heart of resolving some of his issues – and now Mark at least is aware of it, which he wasn't before doing the Map.

Activity 2.4

Leaving aside for the moment a strictly coaching methodology through which Mark could come to suggest for himself what to do next, what do you think are some promising areas to tackle or suggest to Mark that might help him break out of this bind he is in?

We worked in three areas with Mark for six months before he re-mapped his profile. These areas were to do with levels of self-esteem and confidence; more effective time management; and increasing his network of contacts and more networking itself. The rationale for these three areas was quite simple: without higher levels of self-esteem Mark would not have the confidence to change his mode of operation; without more effective time management Mark would never be able to gain discretionary time; and as for the networking it served two distinct functions: to get to know leaders in other organisations[11] so that he could learn from highly successful people at his level what they were doing right, and if the worst came to the worst, to increase his options for employment elsewhere.[12] Simple things were the order of the day: keeping a diary and focusing on logging achievement daily; using the Pareto Principle[13] to prioritise more effectively, weed out low priority activities; attending more prestigious networking events beyond his technical domain and also getting to grips with the power of tools like LinkedIn to associate with aspirational people.

At the end of this period, Mark redid his Motivational Map – and it was immediately obvious how much had changed for him without even his being aware of it. He was aware, of course, that he felt so much better about his work, that there was a renewed confidence in what he was doing, and he had even elicited praise from his boss! So what did his re-drawn Map look like (Figure 2.5)?

Motivational Map summary for Mark's second Map			
Motivator	Position	Score	PMA (/10)
Searcher	1	29	7
Defender	2	24	8
Creator	3	23	4
Expert	4	21	9
Spirit	5	21	5
Director	6	18	4
Builder	7	18	7
Friend	8	15	9
Star	9	11	7
PMA Score	70%		
Cluster Importance			
Relationship (R)	27%		
Achievement (A)	32%		
Growth (G)	41%		

Figures 2.5 Mark's second Motivational Map – 22 numbers

Now the good news is that Mark is 70% motivated and so in the second quadrant (see Figure 2.4) or the Boost Zone. Much higher levels of energy. But note, too, how his motivational profile has changed. It's not that anybody has forced it to happen, but organically he has committed himself to the work of transformation and so has ended up feeling differently about his role. His satisfaction with his levels of autonomy have increased, but not miraculously: they were 3/10 but now they are 5/10. The score of six is average, so there is more to do here, but what is significant is the fact that its importance to his well-being has dropped from first to fifth place. It no longer is bringing him down, and it doesn't count in the calculation of the PMA, only the first three motivators do.

Defender is still second, but wow: his feelings of security have leapt from being 2/10 to being 8/10 – positively good. And true, there is a conflict between Searcher his new top motivator (now decisively so: 29 and Defender only 24, a difference now of five points) and Defender, but given the high satisfaction rating (7/10 and 8/10 respectively) it now appears that the tension between change and resistance to it has been reconciled in the work flow. Switching from Spirit to Searcher usually means a switch from being a loner who has to self-achieve, to being someone who is very customer or client-centric. This may well indicate that the work on networking that we did is really bearing fruit.

Finally, and surprisingly (and one must always allow for surprise in Maps), we find his sixth motivator, Creator, is now his third, and is currently in his top three. It's new, and it's probably scary for Mark: but he wants to innovate, and he probably now needs some directed training to equip him with tools that promote innovation and creativity.

We could go on and comment further, but the point is clear: The Maps enabled a senior leader in a highly successful organisation to begin the turn-around of his performance, and in the first instance through the simple expedient of increasing awareness of what actually motivated him. In working through the Pareto exercises he certainly did free up a bit more time for himself, but the surprising thing was that given that time, he did not then just want more, he wanted to use it more creatively (Creator) and also with more of a client focus (Searcher). Being able to do that, resulted in higher performance and in feelings of being more secure (Defender). Truly, win-win.

But a footnote to all this is, surely: the need to regularly do Maps especially during periods of big changes. In this way we can track what is going on and see what the next steps might be that align with the motivators. And we can go further still in developing leadership self-awareness by considering the leader's own Map in the context of the team's, which they are managing. This, then, becomes really exciting, because we not only see what is driving us but how this stacks up or contrasts with the key-other-people on whom our results depend; this extends our understanding of the leader's self-awareness.

The co-author, Jane Thomas, did some very interesting work on this front with a large and prestigious professional services organisation based in

London, and specifically with their Events team that came under the auspices of the marketing department.

The context is that the previous manager of the events team had been in the role for over 15 years, and two of the team had been in their roles for a similar amount of time. The team had been underperforming for a while, and as they were in the back office of the premises, they did not seem to integrate with the other employees, and their only visibility was when they showed prospective clients around the building for the purpose of its future hire. Indeed, other staff were frequently asking the question: 'What exactly did the Events Department actually do?'

Since this book is about leadership we need to look closely at the profiles of the 'old' and 'new' leaders within the context of mapping motivation in order to see how subtle shifts can make a huge impact.

First, the outgoing leader, Jerry, seemed well motivated (Figure 2.6).

Activity 2.5

What are probably the three most important elements of this Map? What do they mean? What might be the issues arising from them?

Motivational Map Summary for Jerry			
Motivator	Position	Score	PMA (/10)
Defender	1	34	8
Spirit	2	26	7
Searcher	3	26	8
Friend	4	25	8
Builder	5	17	9
Star	6	14	8
Creator	7	13	8
Expert	8	13	7
Director	9	12	8
PMA Score	77%		
Cluster Importance			
Relationship (R)	41%		
Achievement (A)	23%		
Growth (G)	36%		

Figure 2.6 Outgoing leader, Jerry – 22 numbers

Without being dogmatic about it, we would say that first there is the fact that the Relationship-Achievement-Growth type indicators (RAG) scores clearly indicate that Jerry is Relationship dominant (at 41%). This suggests a strong procedural approach to leadership and management, especially as, second, his dominant motivator, Defender, is a strong spike at 34/40. Third, that although he is the leader, taking control (Director) is his lowest motivator! Add to that the learning, Expert, is his second lowest, we potentially have a problem in how he deals with people.

Let's add this now into the mix of his actual team at the time in Figure 2.7.

And let's also see the team without the outgoing leader, how does that compare (see Figure 2.8)?

Activity 2.6

Compare and contrast these two team Maps (Figure 2.7 and Figure 2.8). What do you notice? What might be significant?

Extraordinarily, the Maps are nearly identical: the presence of the leader in a team of only five has not shifted the PMA score at all (still 77%, which means of course the leader is the average of the group), and the rank order of

Name	Defender	Searcher	Friend	Spirit	Builder	Expert	Creator	Star	Director	Motivation Audit	1	2	3
Jerry	34	26	25	26	17	13	13	14	12	77%	8	7	8
Ann	24	17	23	25	27	23	12	17	12	58%	4	9	7
Brenda	29	19	24	23	28	14	16	14	13	87%	9	8	9
Carole	20	30	21	21	14	20	21	12	21	82%	8	9	7
Donna	26	26	22	20	20	18	17	16	15	84%	9	7	9
Total	133	118	115	115	106	88	79	73	73	77%			

TEAM MOTIVATION SCORE	77%	
CHANGE INDEX SCORE	47	
R A G	36	29	35

Figure 2.7 Team Map with outgoing leader
Key: Dark grey – Ist motivator, middle grey – 2nd motivator, light grey – 3rd motivator, textured grey – lowest motivator

Name	Defender	Searcher	Friend	Spirit	Builder	Expert	Creator	Star	Director	Motivation Audit	1	2	3
Ann	24	17	23	25	27	23	12	17	12	58%	4	9	7
Brenda	29	19	24	23	28	14	16	14	13	87%	9	8	9
Carole	20	30	21	21	14	20	21	12	21	82%	8	9	7
Donna	26	26	22	20	20	18	17	16	15	84%	9	7	9
Total	99	92	90	89	89	75	66	61	59	77%			

TEAM MOTIVATION SCORE	77%		
CHANGE INDEX SCORE	42		
R A G	35	31	34

Figure 2.8 Team Map without outgoing leader
Key: Dark grey – 1st motivator, middle grey – 2nd motivator, light grey – 3rd motivator, textured grey – lowest motivator

the motivators is almost the same, except at the bottom end the Star and the Director have changed places: in other words, the presence of the leader has actually depressed the desire to want to take control! Over and above this, the top two motivators are in conflict so far as risk and change are concerned (Defender v Searcher), but clearly the change aversion is currently winning the change battle as Defender is on top, number one.

Not to put too fine a point on it: this is a leadership going nowhere, with employees in a state of stasis; this particularly sad as the leader is blessed with mainly highly motivated (80%+) staff. But this situation had been perpetuated for a long time. When we see both Defender and Friend in the top 3 we have to ask whether the team has become too comfortable: with itself, and with each other, and ultimately is it cruising? Second, given the context of their work – providing high quality environments in which their clients can shine, feel good, or 'star' – one has to query the lowest motivator: Star. Since none of them wishes to 'star' themselves, is the service to the client really optimised? And three, another low one, Director motivator: for three members of staff it seems taking control is their lowest motivator; and the one member, Carol, who wishes to manage is not actually a manager. Clearly, if nothing else, the new leader really must take the reins here. What the co-author actually found exactly mirrored what the Maps were indicating: the team had been allowed to manage themselves and got used to, and liked this way of working; but this had caused them to not meet their annual Events targets, and bookings were also very slow. So motivation, motivators and performance were intimately linked.

Given that the 'old' manager was leaving, the team were anxious about a new manager and the changes that the manager might want to make; from *their* perspective they felt that the team worked well together, although one member had a motivational score of only 58%.

The new Events Leader had a Motivational Map done as part of the recruitment process; this was relevant because the Team Map had been completed previously before the new leader was appointed. On the face of it the new prospective leader was exactly what the team needed. She had a huge amount of experience working in the City, had achieved success in her previous role and so was looking for new challenges, and she appeared highly motivated. What was not to like about that? But what did the Maps say?

Activity 2.7

Compare Jerry's Map (Figure 2.6) with Frieda's (Figure 2.9). What three differences strike you immediately? What implications might these have for the team and team development?

Motivational Map Summary for Frieda			
Motivator	Position	Score	PMA (/10)
Searcher	1	27	8
Creator	2	23	8
Director	3	22	8
Friend	4	21	8
Defender	5	20	8
Spirit	6	20	7
Expert	7	18	8
Star	8	15	7
Builder	9	14	8
PMA Score	80%		
Cluster Importance			
Relationship (R)	31%		
Achievement (A)	30%		
Growth (G)	39%		

Figure 2.9 New leader, Frieda's Map – 22 numbers

First, the RAG scores: Jerry's 21% for Achievement is worryingly low,[14] whereas Frieda's 30% is low but more balanced – there is overall, a much greater desire for risk and change in Frieda's profile. Second, they score similarly for Searcher (26/40 and 27/40 respectively) which is in both their top 3 motivators, but for Frieda it is her most important drive, whereas for Jerry it falls well behind – and so is blunted – by his desire for security. Finally, given we are looking for a team that really needs shaking up, we have the welcome motivator of creativity – innovation – in Frieda's profile. Both of these drives are going to be important if change is really going to happen. But notice, too, as a bonus fourth point: Director is well up in the top 3 for Frieda; there is sometimes a tension between wanting to control and wanting to innovate, but in terms of this team, and the general non-accountability that have developed over time, then wanting to take control is probably a positive motivator in this context. Interestingly, Jerry wants independence – his second motivator – which in a team for which Friend (or belonging) is important may prove counterproductive.

If we now transpose her results into the team we get the following team profile (Figure 2.10).

The new manager, Frieda, was given feedback on her Map profile, and enabled to look at the team's Map profile to see how her profile aligned, matched or contradicted theirs! Immediately the question of leadership came to the fore: who was leading this team? Who wanted to lead the team? Who

Name	Searcher	Defender	Friend	Spirit	Builder	Expert	Creator	Director	Star	Motivation Audit %	1	2	3
Ann	17	24	23	25	27	23	12	12	17	58%	4	9	7
Brenda	19	29	24	23	28	14	16	13	14	87%	9	8	9
Carole	30	20	21	21	14	20	21	21	12	82%	8	9	7
Donna	26	26	22	20	20	18	17	15	16	84%	9	7	9
Leader Frieda	27	20	21	20	14	18	23	22	15	80%	8	8	8
Total	119	119	111	109	103	93	89	83	74	78%			

TEAM MOTIVATION SCORE	78%		
CHANGE INDEX SCORE	49		
RAG	34	31	35

Figure 2.10 New leader, Frieda's Team Map
Key: Dark grey – 1st motivator, middle grey – 2nd motivator, light grey – 3rd motivator, textured grey – lowest motivator

could lead the team? Frieda knew the Service Director expected a clear plan of the team's objectives and how the team was going to meet agreed targets in this new leadership environment.

One obvious line of approach was considering how Carol could be used more effectively: her top 3 motivators were the same as Frieda's and so she too wanted control (Director third motivator), and so might naturally be able to assume more responsibility. But Carol had been in post a long time, had a definite view of how she wanted to expand the Events side of the business, and so might prove challenging if Frieda decided that Carol's ideas were not aligned with Frieda's (and the Service Director's) perception of the business requirements.

But if that was an individual challenge, perhaps even more challenging for Frieda was the realisation (the self-awareness that Maps brought to the table) that she herself was not primarily motivated by security (Defender) or belonging (Friend), though in fact they were fifth and fourth in her motivation hierarchy (and they were scored 20/40 and 21/40 respectively), which meant they were not deep aversions for her. This meant, of course, that she was not likely to be, or want to be part of the 'cosy club' that under-performing relationship motivators can sometimes produce. Before Frieda's arrival, they had all supported each other, and nobody had challenged them about not meeting Events' targets. So beyond the individual challenge was the overall team challenge: which was, how to challenge the failure to meet targets without souring the atmosphere, destroying team motivation such as it was, and simultaneously to meet team expectations whilst fulfilling the organisation's objectives?

Seeing it from the perspective of the motivators, rather than the objectives and targets, was an eye-opener for Frieda. To just insist on achieving objectives would be simply to bulldoze one's way through the people – and undoubtedly in doing so to lose many if not most of them. They were good people; they needed leadership. The starting point was seeing it from their motivational perspective and so building performance from that.

At this point it might be useful to visually summarise some key motivator information that Frieda joining the team immediately produced.

Activity 2.8

Studying Figure 2.11 what would you pick out as being significant data?

The changes in the PMA scores are inconsequential, but two things are important to note here: first, that the team itself, without leadership, is even more resistant to change than with either leader present; this suggests that the 'culture' of the team has taken over in terms of behaviours more deeply than had been suspected. Second, and gratifyingly, the new leader's presence has initiated one small significant shift – perhaps the beginning of something much bigger. Scrutinising the R-A-G scores we see for the first time that the

	PMA %	CHANGE INDEX %	R-A-G
TEAM MAP PREVIOUS LEADER	77	47	36-29-35
TEAM MAP NO LEADER	77	42	35-31-34
TEAM MAP NEW LEADER	78	49	34-31-35

Figure 2.11 3 changing motivational perspectives for the team

Relationship (R) are not dominant: The Growth motivators at 35% are strongest with the new leader. Admittedly, this is not a big or decisive shift in itself (still only 1% ahead), but it is heading in the right direction if change is necessary.

Thus, given what the Maps were telling her, Frieda set up a series of meetings with each team member and sought to – using the Covey phrase[15] – understand before being understood, keeping in mind that she already understood via the Map more than they were aware. In this way she could find out what they were thinking and feeling, checked how that correlated with their Map profile, and then start a dialogue about the key issues for the team: raising its profile and meeting revenue targets.

We need at this point to say we are going to enter more micro-detail about what happened in this situation, and this is because we don't wish to sound like so many books on this topic which read like a fairy tale: '... and they used the Maps, and they all lived happily ever after'. Let's not forget that people are difficult; they have their own issues, and just knowing their motivational profiles isn't necessarily going to be a panacea, especially when, as in this case, 5 people are involved. It only takes one person in a team of any size to make things really awkward, if not downright impossible!

So, Frieda started a series of 1-2-1 meetings which were more positive than she expected; it all seemed full steam ahead. Fortunately, all the while Frieda was still being coached by Jane Thomas. By their third meeting Frieda confessed that she was starting to find certain staff and the way that the team worked frustrating; any suggestions that Frieda made were either ignored or dismissed as 'cannot do'. This really is exactly what the data of Figure 2.11 indicated – a deep change resistance in the employees themselves. She decided to take the team out for lunch to push harder some of her ideas; sadly, as she told Jane subsequently, she forgot to take the Team Map profile with her, and energetically launched into how the future could look and the part that she expected everyone to play. In other words, she failed to use the hot button language of their specific motivators. This resulted in a clash between her and Carol, the member of staff who had the same Map profile as herself. And whilst Carol was obstinate, the rest of the staff would not contribute any ideas. Frieda had left the meeting distressed.

A week later Jane Thomas met with Frieda to help her get her leadership back on track. They decided on the following plan of action, that Frieda would speak with staff individually and understand their reactions from the meeting, as well as expressing her concerns about it.

They responded well to this approach, but she was concerned about the way that their behaviours changed at team meetings, especially if someone didn't like the options discussed.

Step 2, then, was with them to look at:

- What is a team?
- How can a team function effectively together?
- What are the strengths and weaknesses of working as a team, when their roles are quite separate?

Clearly, at this stage it was critical to bring the team together to explore what being a team actually meant; the outcome was that they did feel that they worked as a team, but didn't always require team support to complete the task. Many said that they were individually motivated, which the Map results corroborated. So the question, then, was HOW: how could the team collaborate more effectively? And given the necessary motivation the individuals had, notice the willingness here to try to improve.

Team members agreed that they would look at any crossover of roles and see if this could help them to be more efficient; efficiency was what Frieda wanted to concentrate on. They took the next event and treated it with a collaborative team approach; in analysing the results they found that one member of the team seemed to make a lot of mistakes, which resulted in having a frustrating effect on the rest of the team. This needed more investigation by Frieda with that member of staff. But already this new, collaborative approach was beginning to pay dividends: performance issues with the member of staff were surfacing and starting to be addressed; plus, the whole team started to see the benefits of this approach. They became much more open to ideas and suggestions, and also much less defensive when someone didn't agree with a way forward. The turnaround had started, and it showed in the results: increased efficiency of working, and increased Event bookings.

Activity 2.9

What do you think is the number one lesson for Frieda, for a leader, from this narrative of what actually happened at the professional services organisation?

This was a hard road for their leader, Frieda, but the Maps had served a central function: in, first, beginning to understand her own motivators, and second, in trying to get to grips with other people – those one leads – whose motivators may be different or even similar to one's own. But a key point for the leader is realising that one needs to hold back from implementing one's own dreams, desires, drivers and objectives until one is clear about the motivators of the people being led. To move forward without that is usually to exercise force, and this will inevitably lead to big road blocks along the way. The self-awareness is everything here; and to know oneself is to avoid precipitation and rash action. Chin-Ning Chu[16] said: "Self-observation is essential to self-growth. You must first understand the motives of your own actions in order to understand others". The leader gets to both of these bases!

And finally, how did this affect Frieda motivationally speaking? At the end of the process, when the team were on track and functioning, she did a second Map to see how she had changed. So this is part of a leader's responsibility: to be constantly monitoring and learning about themselves, and making adjustments accordingly.

Motivational Map Summary for Frieda			
Motivator	Position	Score	PMA (/10)
Searcher	1	26	7
Creator	2	23	8
Expert	3	22	7
Director	4	20	8
Star	5	19	7
Defender	6	18	8
Builder	7	18	6
Friend	8	17	8
Spirit	9	17	8
PMA Score	73%		
Cluster Importance			
Relationship (R)	30%		
Achievement (A)	33%		
Growth (G)	37%		

Figure 2.12 Frieda's new Map – 22 numbers

This Map certainly throws up some surprises: first, that at 73% Frieda is less motivated than she was before. Immediately, this signals that perhaps she herself has given so much and now is in need of more support from her own line manager. Is this the beginning of a slow burn-out which needs reversing? Second, the work itself has clearly required her to be more Achievement focused, and this is reflected in the scores: the A- is now 33%, up 3%, and Expert (an Achievement motivator) has replaced Director in her top 3. This perhaps reflects her initial decision to educate the team about what it means to be a team; and also her own ongoing learning about motivation and performance. Lastly, notice how her Friend motivator has become less important to her – in a team of Friends. Clearly, she may be 'friendly' (8/10), but the deeper desire to actually belong has now no place in her emotions: for her it's about getting the job done by making a difference.

This study reveals much about the real-time development of the Self that happens for a leader; at the same time, it covers a lot of ground on the topic of team building: Chapters 6 and 7 have a lot more on this.

Notes

1 Interestingly, the word education comes from the Latin, *educare*, meaning 'to lead forth'.
2 This technique seems to have first been used by Earl Nightingale, co-founder of the Nightingale-Conant Corporation, where his extensive work can be found – https://bit.ly/2z4cL7y.
3 And, of course, this Mindstorming technique can be extended very easily to include others: suppose a whole team or a friend or two is also invited to produce 20 answers to the question of how you could be a better leader over the relevant time frame, then potentially in a short space of time hundreds of potential solutions to a personal or team or organisational problem can be generated. This, then, requires sifting: to sort the best answers from the good answers, and the good from the bad!
4 In *Mapping Motivation*, James Sale, Gower (2016), for example, we list five in Chapter 8: acquiring quality feedback, using diagnostic profiling tools, starting a journal, challenging yourself to leave your 'comfort zone', and 'imagining'.
5 An excellent and more modern exploration of this phenomenon is *How to Befriend your Shadow*, John Monbourquette, Darton, Longman, and Todd (2001).
6 See Wikipedia, https://bit.ly/2tWrGvJ.
7 See https://bit.ly/2u2pgus.
8 In *Motivational Maps* we think there are five active components of quality feedback: 1) Say what THEY said or did, 2) Say positive consequences, 3) Say praise, 4) Say repeat this, and 5) Say you have confidence in them and continued positive consequences; and always be specific, simple and sincere. Of all of these 'saying' components probably expressing what the positive consequences are (number 2) is the most important.
9 The '16' numbers are specifically: the 3 score numbers (out of 10) + the 9 motivator score numbers (out of 40) + the 3 Relationship, Achievement, Growth % scores + the 1 PMA score: a total of 3+9+3+1 = 16 scores.
10 The first map records 16 numbers, but through a system's upgrade his second map included all 22 numbers. The extra 6 numbers are the PMA scores out of 10 for his

fourth (Expert) to his ninth (Star) motivators. This does not materially affect the analysis, although more information is usually better!

11 So, a move away from his professional and 'techy' associations towards the kind of organisations like the county Chamber of Commerce or the Institute of Directors where wider issues of organisational life are at the fore.

12 One of the problems of being on a 'failing' treadmill is the frenetic but entirely insular type of activities that one pursues. The consequence of this is the failure to both see the wider picture or world outside, or to cultivate any meaningful connections outside either. In short, one becomes trapped – exactly what a Spirit most of all detests.

13 The Pareto Principle or 80/20 that establishes that 80% of outcomes usually derive from 20% of inputs. So 80% of inputs are invariably not so important, and not so urgent. For more on the Pareto Principle see Chapter 5 of *Mapping Motivation*, James Sale, Gower (2016) and for even more see Chapter 3 of *Mapping Motivation for Coaching*, ibid.

14 That is worryingly low: consider that control (Director), money (Builder) and expertise (Expert) are the three achievements pillars on which most businesses are built, and so if someone is in a key marketing role, and they do not 'want', or are not driven by any of these things, then there may be an issue.

15 Stephen Covey, *The 7 Habits of Highly Effective People*, Simon and Schuster (2004). Habit 5 says: "Seek First to Understand, Then to Be Understood".

16 Chin-Ning Chu, *Thick Face, Black Heart*, Nicolas Brearley (1997).

Chapter 3

Leadership 360° motivational feedback

In Chapter 2 we looked at how becoming self-aware, and using the Maps to help us, was essential for a leader;[1] we covered the leader considering their own personal map, as stage 1, and then went on to consider how a leader fitted, motivationally, into a team they led, stage 2. Now we come to the third, and most advanced, stage of this process: whereby the leader receives 360° motivational feedback[2] from their team, and these predictive assessments by the team are set alongside the actual result of the leader. Such comparisons can make for fascinating reading!

Before studying a case study from leading Motivational Mappers, Aspirin Business Solutions,[3] it might be wise as well to get an overview of the 360° feedback process, for what we are describing is not the standard fare, but an exciting innovation.

We know that quality feedback is probably the most powerful way known to humans to facilitate enhanced self-awareness; and readers of our earlier book[4] will have learnt of 360° Feedback (or 360° Appraisal). Put simply, this is the systematic method by which employees at certain, regular intervals receive feedback on their performance from a variety of sources: not just their own line manager, but often their colleagues, their subordinates, and even from clients and suppliers, depending on the nature of the organisation. In one obvious sense this has to be a no-brainer: what could be better than someone receiving all this feedback – surely, their performance must improve? You are certainly giving each individual an 'all-round perspective'.[5] Yet for all the hype there are several reasons why 360° Feedback needs to be approached with a long spoon.[6]

The first is the time: it is very time consuming (and so very costly) to set up and run a proper 360° Feedback process. Second, 360° Feedback can become a sad substitute for the real management – engaging management – of employees; instead of managers directly communicating with or holding employees to account, they can use the 360° Feedback as a way of providing negative feedback, whilst at the same time absolving themselves of responsibility for it. Third, the process can sometimes can easily be subverted into one of point-scoring and game-playing within an organisation, and one main

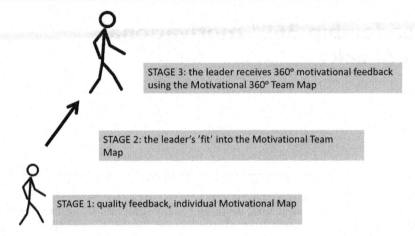

STAGE 3: the leader receives 360° motivational feedback using the Motivational 360° Team Map

STAGE 2: the leader's 'fit' into the Motivational Team Map

STAGE 1: quality feedback, individual Motivational Map

Figure 3.1 Developing motivational self-awareness for leaders: three stages

manifestation of this is when the feedback itself simply becomes a form of necessary 'tick-boxing'. And fourth, in order to set up a trustworthy 360° Feedback system – which is to say, one that is reliable, valid and credible – almost requires a PhD! What one has to understand in order to do this is not your average run-of-the-mill type of competence or understanding. That said, however, the principle that getting feedback from a wide variety of sources is sound. What if Motivational Maps could provide just such 360° Feedback? Fortunately, it can, and can do so quite simply, directly, cheaply[7] and effectively.

The key to doing this is to adapt the Motivational Team Map.[8] In our book *Mapping Motivation for Engagement* we considered an employee, whom we called E, and created a team map charting not only E's Motivational Map, but how other team members, including the leader of the team, saw E from a motivational perspective. That is to say, based on how they perceived E's motivation based on E's actions and words. Here what we want to do is to take this a stage further, and consider not just an employee, but the leader as the focus of the team Motivational Map. What perceptions do employees have of their leader from a motivational perspective? Do these accord with the leader's own self-perceptions? How does this help the leader become more effective, more productive, a better leader?

Activity 3.1

In your view, how might knowing what your team members think your motivational profile is, help your leadership capacity? How would it help you become a better leader?

Figure 3.2 Susannah Brade-Waring and Heath Waring celebrate

Understanding how people perceive you, especially motivationally, which is to say emotionally, is vitally important. First, it is going to help the leader anticipate problems that derive from false expectations. For example, if staff generally perceive that their leader is driven by a particular motivator, say Star or Builder or Searcher,[9] then if, especially, this motivator is not important to them,[10] then they will seek confirmatory bias.[11] In other words, as you take centre stage (Star), insist upon financial results (Builder) or talk about a better world tomorrow (Searcher), they will consciously or otherwise 'discount' that desire (or want or motivator) that you have because they will see it as simply your ego speaking rather than something of objective significance that they can buy into. Furthermore, they will keep looking for evidence that this is indeed how their leader is. In short, the leader's own credibility is undermined by not understanding how their employees see them!

Second, by understanding how they see you motivationally, you are able (and this as subtly as you want) to counter the stereotyping that their beliefs create about you. So if, for example, there is a perception that you are a Star – and like the limelight – the leader, then, has the opportunity to quite explicitly not take prime or pole position at every meeting or event, but to allow others to assume the spotlight. Over time employees may forget that they ever thought their leader was a Star (or any other motivator) and come to a realisation that the leader is there for them, because their behaviours and words demonstrate that fact. Again, then, this is important because it is giving the leader more 'control' but not in the traditional 'command-and-control' manner which has become so outdated and counterproductive in the best contemporary organisations.

Third, it is important that staff do understand what the leader's true motivators are, and that there is no ambiguity about it. In that way, the leader can
be nourished and sustained by their employees, just as their primary purpose
is to nourish and sustain the team and each member of it. This is really all
about clarity of communication. We all 'get' what that means when clarity of
goals, or clarity of language, is the point at issue; but it's equally important
for people to 'get' where we are coming from emotionally, motivationally. The
semantics of our communications are really only 7%'s worth of their impact;
the Non Verbal Communication (NVC) component is usually some 93%'s
worth.[12] But this 93% conveys both our emotional and ethical states; by
which we mean that from it our employees can estimate whether or not we
are speaking from our hearts (how we really feel) and from our true values
(our ethics). In other words, whether we are credible and trustworthy. For
staff to know we are credible and trustworthy is far more important than
anything we have to say about what we are doing, in the sense that nobody is
listening to what we need to do if the speaker – the leader – is not credible
and not trustworthy. It should be pretty clear, then, that we cannot over-
estimate how important a 360° Team Motivational Map is for the leader.

Susannah Brade-Waring of Aspirin Business Solutions took all this on
board with her client, Lee,[13] a leader in a well-known, major, national super-
market chain. And additionally, Susannah was particularly keen on identifying what she called the 'blind spots' in a leader's motivations, and
corresponding behaviours, which can lead to sub-optimal performance. Citing
Tony Robbins,[14] "Whatever people do, they have a reason. They may not
know what that reason is – at least not consciously", Susannah observed that
people did tend to excel in behaviours that derived from their motivators and
fitted their values, but where there was a 'blind spot' or spots, then it was
crucial not only to seek the seek and understand the feedback, but also to act
upon it. If that could be done, then the potential for 360° Motivational
Mapping to unleash the full potential of leaders would be almost unlimited.
But whereas we can see the value of receiving feedback from other people, it's
often noted that leaders and managers rarely ask or look for it. Again, they
do look for tangible measures, such as KPIs[15] or trends in data; and they may

Figure 3.3 Three benefits of understanding employee motivators – leader's perspective

even notice things don't 'feel' right in the office. However, to ask for others' opinions about oneself can be challenging and demotivating. The information may be inaccurate, ill-informed or biased. We might not like what we hear. And, perhaps worst of all, we might not want to change our behaviour. All in all, for many leaders, data is a much faster, accurate and less painful way to assess and measure what is going on.

This makes sense – both logically and emotionally. Robert Cialdini said,[16] "You and I exist in an extraordinarily complicated stimulus environment, easily the most rapidly moving and complex that has ever existed on this planet. To deal with it, we need shortcuts". The word 'hack' has become part of our everyday language. Leaders are encouraged to run 'sprints'[17] or 'hackathons' where organisations, including the likes of the biggest such as Apple, Google and Amazon, bring people together in a competitive environment to find breakthrough solutions quickly. In short, we're increasingly motivated to find the quickest way to our outcome.[18]

Given this, what has it to do with 360° feedback? Simply, that sooner or later, successful managers and leaders realise that shortcuts (or 'hacks'!) don't work with people – at least not for sustainable and outstanding performance. A technology – or a methodology – or a process, as it were – that works so well in so many other areas of business or organisational life, does not work so well here; 'here' being arguably the most important place of all – the people, the staff, the very life of the organisation. So providing someone with a clear job description, fair pay and the resources to do their job is just not enough. Annual appraisals don't work either, according to research by The Chartered Institute of Personnel and Development (CIPD), which found that almost three-quarters of senior leaders from outside HR considered annual appraisals ineffective.[19]

If appraisals don't inspire people or drive performance, what does? Unsurprisingly, for those following the thread of our argument, the CIPD recommends regular conversations with good quality feedback and appropriate staff development. This means staff need to be actively engaged in evaluating and developing their own performance, and this requires managers and leaders to know how to engage and motivate their teams – what makes them tick? What will engage and drive their performance to go the extra mile, to want excellence for themselves and their organisation? And, for those leaders and managers who truly want to excel, 'How I am influencing that?'

Good quality feedback, then – again – is essential for improving performance. 360° feedback offers line managers a wide-ranging perspective, helping to make performance management a more objective and fair process. (180° feedback[20] for non-line managers can also be very effective for the same reasons.)

Thus, the only really outstanding issue in undertaking a 360° feedback process is how we do it; in other words, via which methodology? For we have already said that for it to be done well the traditional 360° process is a costly and time-consuming exercise. The danger is that all too often, 360°s demotivate people and create disengagement. They can lead to key people feeling underappreciated. They can damage relationships. And they can be used by managers as a way to ensure their managers receive negative feedback, without taking responsibility for having those challenging conversations themselves. All of which ultimately results in reduced collaboration, innovation, performance and profits.

How then can such valuable feedback be provided without demotivating or disengaging people?

Activity 3.2

Ask yourself the same question: how would you provide valuable feedback to your employees, or indeed to anyone, without potentially demotivating or disengaging them from you?

Aspirin Business Solutions took this issue very seriously. They began by trialling a 'softer' 360° Feedback process using a four-colour personality profiling tool, which appeared to be superior, especially in affirming positive traits. But although feedback was received more openly, employees seemed unconvinced or unmoved to take action. The feedback was too general to be actionable.

Aspirin Business Solutions then learnt of Mark Turner's[21] piloting Motivational Maps as a 360° feedback tool,[22] and intrigued, trialled it themselves. The results were both surprising and encouraging – in both the depth of the insights and how easy it was for leaders to take the feedback on board. The significant cost savings[23] were both a bonus and an enabler. The client chosen to undertake the project was extremely willing to do the pilot because they had already experienced the Mapping tool and been coached upon its results. Thus, there was already, it has to be said, a liking, trust and understanding, which made acceptance, and so progress, fluid and easy.

With this in mind, Aspirin Business Solutions devised a leadership programme using Mapping Motivation's 360° Feedback Process for Lee, their client. Already, reviewing his Personal Development Plan, Lee was keen to develop his potential, including his mind-set, behaviours, knowledge and skills. A bespoke programme of 12-months' duration was in operation, and was going well, but half-way through Aspirin discussed the benefits to Lee of 360° feedback from his colleagues. This would provide in-depth information enabling Lee to:

- better assess his own behaviours, communication skills and personal impact
- identify if the improvement in delivering his KPIs was damaging his relationships with his colleagues, thereby disengaging fellow colleagues
- identify specific ways to strengthen these relationships, and
- improve his relationship-building, influencing and engagement skills.

Lee asked for Motivational Map feedback from six colleagues at his company. These included two of his team (name: Team 1 and 2), his direct manager (name: Manager 1), the head of his department (name: Manager 2) and two internal customers (name: Customers 1 and 2). In addition to a request in-person, they were emailed instructions – see Figures 3.4 and 3.5.

As a result of the 360° feedback from the six nominated colleagues/internal customers, along with Lee's own Motivational Map, the following 'Team' report was compiled.

Dear _____

You will receive an email today from Motivational Maps.

This links to a specific profile which is a different approach to 360°. It is based on identifying the underlying motivators which drive my behaviour. Click on the link – and follow the instructions BUT base your answers on me, as we are adapting how the Map is being used.

There are 2 sets of questions. In the first set, you'll be asked to pick which of the two statements offered, best represents my preferences based on what you know of me (my behaviour, apparent priorities, etc.). See Figure 3.5 below. There are no right or wrong answers, and all respondent's answers will be compiled and anonymised. If you're happy for me to know your responses, please let me know. The second set of questions simply asks you to rate, out of 10, how motivated you think I am in each of the nine motivators.

I will keep you updated on this, as I incorporate the 360° feedback into my Personal Development Plan. Please complete at your earliest convenience, and ideally within one week? The questionnaire takes around 15 minutes to complete when undisturbed.

Thank you

Lee

Figure 3.4 Instructions and screenshot for completing 360° Feedback Motivational Map

Please remember to answer both sets of questions on Lee

- There are 36 statements grouped into pairs
- Use the option buttons between the two statements to indicate which statement is more like Lee
- The closer to a statement you select the option button, the more you feel it is like Lee

EXAMPLE

| Lee wants to be highly skilled in what he does | ( ) ( ) (x) ( ) ( ) | Lee wants to have a reputation |

Figure 3.5 36 Paired statements: first set of questions

Activity 3.3

Study the data in Figure 3.6. Keep in mind that only Lee's map numbers are a self-assessment: the other numbers from Team member number 1 to internal customer number 2 are all fellow colleagues and their motivational perspectives on Lee. What do you think are the three most significant items about Lee's own map that emerge from studying this data?

Possibly the three most significant aspects of Lee's map are:

1 That he is in the second quadrant of motivation, the Boost Zone,[24] and so some small steps or tweaks could enable him to be fully in the Optimal Zone of motivation (which is 80%+).
2 That the Searcher motivator, whilst being his most important motivator, is also the one he is least satisfied by – only 7/10 – and so this is the most critical area to focus on if Lee is going to increase his motivation and so his performance levels as a leader.
3 That there is an internal conflict between the pull or direction of the motivators: Searcher and Creator are risk and change friendly, whereas Defender is risk and change averse. So the question becomes: does this generate any issues for Lee – for example, issues of indecision, procrastination, and lack of clarity? Clearly, as a leader, the opposites – decisiveness, speed and clarity – are vitally important.[25]

	Searcher	Defender	Director	Creator	Spirit	Expert	Builder	Friend	Star	Motivation Audit %	1	2	3
Team 1	24	22	23	19	18	21	19	15	19	96%	10	9	9
Team 2	31	23	18	21	17	21	19	9	21	59%	5	7	8
Manager 1	29	21	27	19	18	13	30	9	14	89%	9	9	8
Manager 2	27	23	15	17	19	24	19	21	15	90%	9	9	9
Customer 1	28	21	20	20	23	15	10	28	15	90%	9	9	9
Customer 2	35	16	25	26	24	17	13	13	11	80%	8	8	8
Lee	29	27	21	22	16	20	18	16	11	75%	7	8	9
Total	203	153	149	144	135	131	128	111	106	82%			

Figure 3.6 360° Motivational feedback to the leader
Key: Dark grey – 1st motivator, middle grey – 2nd motivator, light grey – 3rd motivator, textured grey – lowest motivator

Activity 3.4

Now consider what are the three most significant items of feedback that emerge from his colleagues? List what you think are the most significant three issues.

There are far more than three significant items that emerge for Lee when we look at these numbers; there is indeed a wealth of information. But let's consider three things initially.

1   He underrates his own motivation compared with most (barring the Team 2 member) of his assessors; thus, Lee is putting on a good show at work, which as a leader is a necessary aspect of leadership work.[26]

2   Lee's self-assessment is close to his assessors' view of him, as all predict his Searcher motivator, and 50% predict his Defender motivator. This suggests that Lee is reasonably transparent and consistent in his behaviours to his colleagues.

3   But Lee is also a Creator (at this time) and only one other assessor sees that; three, indeed, see a conflicting motivator, Director, as being more important to Lee.

What does this mean? How does this help Lee grow as a leader?

Before answering these questions and outlining the feedback that Aspirin actually gave back to Lee, let's identify some further issues that the numbers suggest.

1   Team member 2 is clearly problematic, and this needs examining. How do we know this? They perceive Lee as only 59% motivated (in the Risk Zone[27]), whereas everyone else (apart from Lee himself) perceives Lee as in the Optimal Zone of motivation. Indeed, were Team 2 not in the team, then the overall motivational score would be perceived as 89%, very high in fact. Even more significantly, Team 2 sees Lee's lowest motivator as one of Lee's top 3; also views the Friend motivator as Lee's lowest; and finally, although correctly identifying Lee's top motivator as the Searcher, yet sees that as being his least effectively realised motivator (5/10). The net effect of all these numbers is to suggest that: team member 2 sees Lee as an unfriendly, perhaps mildly narcissistic, and a not particularly able leader; they, therefore, see Lee as relatively de-motivated as a result.

2   Lee is perceived by his team as a 'safe pair of hands'. Only Customer 2 has scored his Defender motivator less than 20/40, and even 16/40 is not terribly low. So although for Manager 1 and Customer 1 Defender is not in their attributed top 3, yet their scores above 20 suggest they recognise that Lee is efficient and wants to get things right.

3   Lee has scored Director above 20, so it is important, though not one of his top 3. Three team members, however, perceive Lee as wanting to

wield authority as a top 3 motivator; this is compounded in complexity by the almost equally strong perception (149 v. 144) that Lee wants to innovate. Lee does want to innovate but only one member of the team, Customer 2, actually positions it in Lee's top 3. Keep in mind that Director and Creator are generally conflicting motivators,[28] then we have an issue as to whether Lee is conveying the right message: is he perceived as too controlling? Or, are we as a team innovating enough? Or actually has the right balance between control and creativity[29] been struck?

4   As we often like to observe, lowest motivators can reveal fascinating data: in this instance there is a conflicting perception as three of Lee's colleagues perceive Friend to be Lee's lowest motivator, whilst one perceives it to be his top motivator. This would suggest that for Customer 1 (28/40) Lee has a particularly warm relationship, but keep in mind that Customer 1 is an internal customer and not a core part of his team. The team itself and one manager see Friend as Lee's lowest, and two of them have Friend's polarity reinforcement,[30] the Director, in the top 3. Perhaps here Lee needs to spend a little more time in showing he cares! The degree of caring he needs to demonstrate will depend on the actual team map of the real team (that is to say, not on the feedback map based on their perceptions of Lee).In feeding these points back to Lee, how does he respond?

a   Lee is succeeding in conveying to his team that he is highly motivated. A perceived motivation score of 84%[31] puts Lee in the Optimal Zone of motivation, which is described as having lots of energy, enthusiasm and resilience (and, incidentally, is high compared with other leaders mapped in other organisations). Lee is happy with this and needs to sustain what he is already doing.

b   Also, his desire to make a difference comes across very clearly and he can use this common understanding and desire when communicating. Furthermore, overall his colleagues, bar one, have a good understanding of what motivates him and are likely therefore to understand him.

c   The one team member who perceives Lee as poorly motivated is someone who Lee talks to more frequently and openly. So, Lee is now aware that his conversations may be leading to a misperception which could be unsettling his team, and he will address this. Note here, especially, that the analysis from the numbers alone in Point 4 above are now 'corrected' by speaking to the client – whereas we assumed in reading the numbers that there was a problem with Team 2 member, Lee makes it clear that the problem stems from his own too liberal communication with Team 2, and so this has had, inadvertently, a de-motivating effect.[32]

d   Whilst Lee does not seek friendship at work, he is disappointed that some colleagues may feel he avoids them, and possibly discounts values such as collaboration, inclusivity and helping people feel significant; all aspects of employee engagement. He decides to invest more time in finding a more effective balance and leadership style.

e   Finding this effective balance and leadership style is helped by seeing how the team members perceive him: where there are matches in profile, Lee sees how he can build on this – for example, Customer 2 shares the Creator motivator perception with Lee as well as the lowest Star motivator, suggesting that he/she gets where Lee is coming from; equally, where there is a mismatch Lee can consciously adjust his behaviour and style to suit that colleague's preference – for example, one of his managers (Manager 2) perceives the Director motivator to be Lee's lowest. Is his manager looking for evidence of a different leadership style from Lee, e.g. one that he values himself? Indeed, this then led to a good conversation with that manager about leadership styles.

Activity 3.5

Given the points a) to e) above, what do you think are the most important outcomes of using a 360 Motivational Team Map? Make a list of the key benefits.

In summary, as a methodology for 360° feedback, Lee felt the insights he gained were intriguing and profound. He was motivated to learn more and

'360° feedback using Motivational Maps'

We experienced the following outcomes:

- Employees/Leaders are curious and want to understand more.

- Employees/Leaders can 'see' how their colleagues perceive their behaviour, in a non-threatening way.

- Based on the feedback, employees/leaders identify the outcomes they desire, and ways to change their behaviour.

- Increased awareness of other's motivators: Employees/Leaders are able to see how their colleagues' own motivators influence how they perceive others' behaviours. This increases their awareness of their colleagues' motivators, personality and preferences.

- Situational Leadership: Employees/Leaders can observe how they adjust their own behaviour to suit others' personalities and roles. They can also see how successful this is based on the feedback.

Figure 3.7 Outcomes from using 360° feedback with Motivational Maps

gratified to see confirmation of his efforts. As the feedback is based on perceptions of Lee's motivators, he did not feel threatened or unappreciated. The input of six colleagues input provided him with a well-rounded view.

The follow-on from these results is also worth commenting on. Lee has been promoted to cover for a secondment in a key role. It is a significant move in terms of responsibility, role and geographic location. Lee's investment in developing strong relationships with his colleagues has enabled this move to go far more smoothly than one might expect. One of his team members has been promoted to cover Lee's role, and this has been openly accepted by their clients. Lee now has a better understanding of their emotional as well as technical needs and is able to have more open discussions about how he can best support these within his new role. Lee's next focus is to strengthen his relationships with his new team and, of course, he's looking to Motivational Maps to provide valued insights. But essential to all this success – lest we forget – is Lee's own motivation to improve his performance. This fits beautifully with his Searcher motivator which, above all, seeks feedback on the difference he's making. Peter Drucker said, "What gets measured gets managed"[33] and 360° Feedback via Motivational Maps provides both tangible measures and feedback Lee believes in. And so, inevitably, he wanted to improve his team and himself. That made all the difference.

This use of Motivational Maps 360° Team feedback has been very detailed and analytic, but we think necessarily so, because it is so important in the development of leadership. In Chapter 7 we use another case study to show again how this can be used, but in a less successful situation. And as we conclude this chapter let us remind ourselves of where we are because this Map 360° Team feedback has taken us on a long journey: the 4+1 model leadership starts by us understanding that the development of the self is core to all that the leader is and can become. Self-awareness is the root of that journey for developing the Self. Feedback is the basis of self-awareness and Motivational Maps initiates just such self-awareness in a new and multi-layered way.

Notes

1 And the importance of leadership is: "Senior leadership is regarded as the most critical driver of sustainability within a business and nearly half of businesses (44%) believe engagement with business leaders will be the most important factor in successfully implementing a sustainability strategy over the next three years" – Economist Intelligence Unit (EIU) and Coca-Cola Enterprises, Sustainability Insights: *Learning from Business Leaders*, 2013; also, "Deloitte found that companies viewed as having particularly strong leadership could enjoy a stock market valuation premium of more than 15 per cent. Those seen as having ineffective leadership suffered discounts of up to 20 per cent" – David Wighton, Investors agree that quality of leadership is crucial for high performance, *The Times*, 12 June 2012.

2 The first use of the Motivational Map for 360° Feedback was devised by Mark Turner of Motivational Maps Education Ltd. More can be found about his case study in *Mapping Motivation for Engagement*, Routledge (2018).

3 Aspirin Business Solutions can be found at https://bit.ly/2DItM7o.
4 James Sale and Steve Jones, *Mapping Motivation for Engagement*, Routledge (2018), Chapter 6.
5 A phrase used by a leading UK expert on 360° Feedback: Elva R Ainsworth. Her book, *360° Feedback: A Transformational Approach*, Panoma Press (2016), is an extremely insightful and valuable contribution in this field.
6 We do, of course, in the *Mapping Motivation for Engagement* book provide a positive spin on 360° feedback too!
7 This application is still in its early days of experimentation within the Maps' community, but anecdotal evidence from practitioners using this methodology suggest that it is some 70% less in terms of cost, and even better still in terms of time saved.
8 The first Mapper to do this and to whom we are indebted for this idea and case study of E is Mark Turner – http://bit.ly/2pe2iAH.
9 Any of the nine motivators could be cited here, but we have just chosen three for the purposes of illustration.
10 Of course, if the motivator is important to them, that is, if they – the majority – share the motivator with the leader, then there will tend to be an unthinking and unquestioning assumption that all is well or that all is 'normal'; and as we know, when everybody thinks the same, then nobody is thinking at all. Which, from a leadership perspective is also very dangerous.
11 According to Wikipedia "Confirmation bias, also called confirmatory bias or myside bias, is the tendency to search for, interpret, favour, and recall information in a way that confirms one's pre-existing beliefs or hypotheses. It is a type of cognitive bias and a systematic error of inductive reasoning".
12 Albert Mehrabian, *Nonverbal Communication*, Aldine Transaction (2007).
13 We have anonymised the name of the leader and the company in order to ensure confidentiality.
14 https://bit.ly/2DItM7o
15 KPI – Key Performance Indicators
16 Robert Cialdini, *Influence: The Psychology of Persuasion*, Harper Business (2007).
17 Indeed, a great example of this is contained in the best-selling book, *Sprint: How To Solve Big Problems and Test New Ideas in Just Five Days*, by Jake Knapp, John Zeratsky, and Braden Kowitz, Bantam Press (2016), and whose sub-title says it all. The ideas in this book primarily come from their experiences at Google Ventures.
18 Edward Deci observed, "Research has shown that when employees get focussed on rewards, their tendency is to take the shortest path to the outcomes" from *The Oxford Handbook of Work Engagement, Motivation, and Self-Determination Theory*, OUP USA (2014).
19 https://bit.ly/2FY7wJ8
20 To be clear here: 360° feedback is where the 'feedbackers' (sometimes called 'raters') include people at all levels of relationship with the subject; that could be superiors, subordinates or direct reports, peers/colleagues, or even external customers or suppliers. A 180° feedback, on the other hand, is where the 'feedbackers' are at the same level as the subject (peers or colleagues), and a person they report to.
21 Ibid, Endnote vii.
22 For the first specific case study that Mark Turner produced, see *Mapping Motivation for Engagement*, James Sale and Steve Jones, Routledge (2018), Chapter 6.
23 When we say 'enabler' here what we actually mean is that given that Mark's client was an educational institution, the cost savings were such that without this process no 360° feedback project would have been affordable at all! Those who work in the

public sector, and the private sector which complements it, will immediately understand the importance of this observation.

24 For a full discussion of the meaning of the four Zones of motivation, see *Mapping Motivation*, James Sale, Routledge (2016), Chapter 4.

25 We need to be clear here: Lee is an excellent leader and in this role his primary purpose is risk management, so that Defender is a highly appropriate motivator, and he is innovative in his approach to how the risk is managed; furthermore, he is a senior manager – leader – in a very large organisation that has existed for over 100 years, so although we are talking of speed and decisiveness here, practically we are all aware that in such organisations one is constrained – fogged even – by the layers of management and strategy that have necessarily accrued over the years.

26 It is a central principle of our work that the leader's motivation must be greater than the average motivation of his immediate team; for if it is not, why need the team members be bothered?

27 *Mapping Motivation*, ibid.

28 For more on conflicting motivators see *Mapping Motivation for Coaching*, James Sale and Bevis Moynan, Routledge (2018), Chapter 8.

29 Control (Director motivator) tends to inhibit creativity (Creator motivator); just as creativity tends to innovate and produce 'structures' that are not controllable by the original authority, since they oftentimes fall outside of its jurisdiction. The internet, for example, is a classic example of a 'new' product that even nation State authorities have trouble controlling; and all accounts of creativity seem to emphasise how freedom/play, not control, are essential for full creativity to be realised. As Teresa Amabile put it, "Intrinsic motivation is conducive to creativity; extrinsic motivation is detrimental to creativity". And the consequences of all this 'external motivation' are best described by Gary Hamel: "Finally, and worst of all, industrialisation disconnected employees from their own creativity". *The Future of Management*, Harvard Business School Press (2007).

30 For much more on 'polarity reinforcement' see *Mapping Motivation for Coaching*, ibid., Chapter 6.

31 The team table says 82%, but that includes Lee's score of 75%, which is not of course a 'perceived' score, but Lee's actual score. So removing it from the calculation actually increases the perceived score for him.

32 This is a salutary antidote to the idea that we often espouse that being open and candid with colleagues and staff is usually the best option, and that 'disclosure' often builds trust. All that is true, but the other side of the coin is that sometimes as leaders we have to hold back, refrain from telling everything, especially our anxieties and worries, since these things can be misconstrued as doubts – which can become toxic and infectious, and undermine any enterprise. Context, again, is everything.

33 Peter Drucker, *The Effective Executive*, Routledge (2007). It is worth commenting that this quotation is often taken out of context, as Drucker was also fully aware that some vital aspects of work were not actually measurable.

Chapter 4

Leaders thinking and planning

We saw in Chapter 1 that Motivational Maps adopts a pragmatic approach to leadership that it calls the '4+1' model. Chapters 2 and 3 explored how the root of self-development could be developed through a three-step process (Figure 3.1) using Mapping Motivation; that was the '+1' of the model. It might be good to remind ourselves of this model and also to do a quick evaluation alongside it. The '4+1' domains are: self-development (+1), Thinking (1), Doing (2), Team building (3) and Motivating (4). If we identify two key processes in each of these 5 domains, then we have 10 categories:

		I rate myself as... (/10)
SELF	Self-awareness Self-development	
THINKING	Values Strategizing	
DOING	Recruiting Appraising	
TEAM BUILDING	Motivational Team audits Team language and communication	
MOTIVATING	Motivational Personal audits Motivational reward strategies	
	TOTAL	%

Figure 4.1 Measuring yourself against the '4+1' model

Activity 4.1

Study Figure 4.1 and ask yourself how well you perform at each of the categories: how self-aware are you, how much self-development do you undertake? How clear are you about your organisation's values and your own leadership ones? How effectively do you strategize? How good are you at recruiting high-performing employees? And how well do you undertake performance appraisals – do they actually boost performance? Similarly, how often do you consider auditing your team from a motivational perspective? Is there a common team language that enables the process of working together to be smooth and not bogged down in personality conflicts and misunderstandings?[1] Is the motivation of individuals taken into account and regularly audited? How well are your rewards aligned with the motivations of your staff? Give yourself a score out of 10 (maximum, and 1 minimum) for each of these categories. Tally your scores for an overall percentage.

This, clearly, is a rough and ready way of seeing how you are currently doing, and we have limited the test to those areas where motivation (and mapping) is especially relevant. That said, if you do it honestly, you will find that it provides some useful information.

First, what your overall level of performance as a leader is likely to be; this is important because it is a benchmark from which one can build and improve. As with Map scores we take the view that performance falls into four levels[2] and so in considering your score where are you (see Figure 2.4 to remind yourself of the categories)?

To translate these quadrants into practical ideas: The Optimal Zone means that if you have scored yourself 80% or above, then as a leader you are performing at a high level. The issue for you, then, is how do you maintain it? (Another issue will be point 3 below). Alternatively, if you are in the Boost Zone, some targeted tweaking – specific developments in one or of the '4+1' domains will be in order. On the other hand, if you are below the threshold score of 60%, then some serious development and changes will be necessary if you are to become a high-performing leader; the issue for you will be where to start on the re-equipping of yourself as a leader? Finally, if you are below 35% in your scoring, you will know yourself that not much can be going right for you in your leadership practice: you will experience a sense of confusion and anxiety (through lack of self-awareness), mixed results at best (through lack of effective strategizing), people problems (through poor recruitment and ineffectual management processes), team disintegration (through lack of coherent communication, amongst other things) and staff disenchantment and disengagement – working to rule (through lack of understanding their motivators).

Second, what your strengths are. Look for scores of eight or more. Indeed, what is your strongest asset as a leader? Any asset, of course, taken to an extreme without reference to the other domains will become a liability. For example, all the greatest 'thinking' in the world without the ability to implement ('doing') is futile; and equally, great implementation skills without sufficient thought as to what is important and needs to be done is also highly dangerous, as it leads to building houses on sand! But, given your strongest asset, rejoice in it – that is a unique feature you have, and in identifying it very specifically in this way, we are increasing self-awareness of its importance and value to the organisation, and also to you personally. There is always a case for developing our strengths so that they are stronger; till, in fact, we become pre-eminent in the exercise of them.

Third, and what is your lowest score, your potentially weakest area of performance? This is presumably your Achilles' Heel – the point at which you are vulnerable. It is worth considering how a serious weakness in any area of leadership capability might affect results.

Activity 4.2

If my score for any of the '4+1' qualities were three or less, what problems might that cause? See Figure 4.2.

Let's consider some more obvious implications of low scores in these five areas. Lack of self-development would mean, ultimately, less confidence, less resilience, and almost certainly result in the attempt to solve today's issues with yesterday's knowledge and skills. Poor thinking will lead to crucial strategic mistakes, which will be catastrophic for an organisation. Weak implementation will create quality and consistency issues for the customer or client, as well as being demoralising for other staff. Failure to build strong teams must impact performance and productivity – so ultimately profits or value. And finally, failure to reward appropriately will be de-motivating and result in disengagement; again to the detriment of overall results.

Activity 4.3

Given the above concerns and ideas, what actions are you going to take in order to improve your leadership capabilities? Where do you need to develop greater skills and abilities? How are you going to do this and over what time frame? Finally, how will you know you have been successful?

Now we need to move on to consider the four specific skills[3] that we identified as crucial. The first of these is 'Thinking' and obviously this – like the others – is a huge area. But keep in mind, our interest always is how motivation impacts thinking or how we can think better using motivation or Motivational Maps' tools. We saw in Chapter 1 that 'leadership thinking about an organisation' looked like Figure 1.4. Leaders had to think about issues such as values, vision, mission, strategy, plans, goals, innovation and, more generally, problem-solving. More 'generally' because solving problems is the order of the day, virtually every day; there is always some problem for an organisation to solve;[4] and the mind that 'thinks' is always attempting to anticipate these problems in advance. But keep in mind here, too, whilst we are shortly going to share a new Motivational Maps tool that is a problem-solving device, motivation is highly relevant to problem-solving in the broadest sense. How? Because solving problems requires immense amounts of energy, and energy is

'4+1' QUALITY	If my score were 3 or less, this might cause...
SELF-AWARENESS/SELF-DEVELOPMENT	
THINKING/STRATEGIZING	
DOING/IMPLEMENTING	
TEAM BUILDING/COMMUNICATING	
MOTIVATING/REWARDING	

Figure 4.2 Problems if '4+1' scores three or less

motivation. Without energy – motivation – the mind wilts as one problem after another stacks up, and ultimately one experiences burnout[5] with the overload. So, it is absolutely necessary to maintain motivational levels as a leader. And, of course, high levels of energy inspire others too.

In our book, *Mapping Motivation for Engagement*,[6] we looked at the strategic narrative necessary to drive an organisation successfully, and how the Motivational Organisational Map could be used to help align values and develop talent. We are not going to repeat that information, though clearly it is relevant to effective leadership; instead, we want to drop down a notch, a level, to consider the planning process which is also critical for the leader.

Activity 4.4

Here is a good question for you: when considering your annual holiday or vacation, what is the first question that pops into your mind? Write it down immediately, and do not second guess your answer.

We have found that there are typically five responses to this question; and usually one's answer reveals something about one's type of focus. This 'type of focus' is important as a leader, since we first need to become aware of our own preferences, and second to realise that whatever our own focus is (which, incidentally, over a prolonged period tends to be a strength, but a strength that generates a corresponding weakness or Achilles' Heel). So which of these five questions occurred to you?

In these questions, applied to an annual vacation, we clearly have a planning device or heuristic tool to enable us to problem-solve, which is as much as to say, to cope with change. This is The Five Elements Model[7] and it provides the leader with a systematic process to enable them to plan any project large or small: from the future of the whole organisation over the next five years to where am I going on vacation next year?

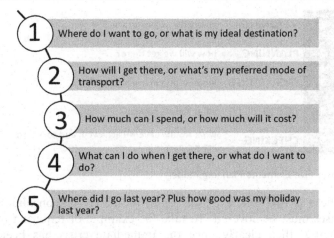

Figure 4.3 Five questions surrounding holidays

If we consider this small project, we see how the five steps are inter-connected. Consider the following responses to the questions:

1 My ideal destination is Sydney Australia (and I am based in the UK)
2 By train; I hate flying
3 My bank account is currently £2K overdrawn and I have no savings
4 I love seeing Renaissance art and visiting Gothic churches
5 Bognor Regis – terrible; it rained so much that most of my time I stayed in

Clearly, there is a mismatch in this (imaginary) planning scenario that one scarcely knows where to begin to sort! But whilst it seems ridiculous from a holiday planning point of view, it is not so ridiculous when we review it from how organisations really do plan – namely, badly. To take one response only, the first, how many organisations fail[8] because they have an absurdly grand-iose vision of where they are going to be, and at the same time no sense of a detailed plan, adequate resourcing, decisive action or proper monitoring of how they are succeeding? There, we have it! The five key elements, but now in more organisational-friendly language.

A number of points need to be made about this model before we expand it. First, we use the gerund, or verbal-noun, form of the word rather than simply the noun. In other words, we prefer to say 'visioning' rather than 'vision', since the gerund implies action.[9] This is an action model, not an academic framework.[10] Second, the starting point may not necessarily be the Visioning, or point 1. Often organisations like to kick off with the last question in the cycle: Where are we now? But equally, circumstances can dictate we begin anywhere: a crisis, for example, might precipitate us into asking 'what actions need to happen – NOW!' The idea

1	VISIONING	where do we want to be?
2	PLANNING	how will we get there?
3	FACILITATING	what resources are necessary?
4	DOING	what actions happen?
5	CHECKING	what results have we achieved, and so, where are we now?

Figure 4.4 The Five Elements Planning Model

to grasp here is that wherever we begin, ultimately to consolidate success all five bases must be covered. To take the example of requiring immediate action, Doing, then clearly once the immediate crisis has been ameliorated, then we will need to consider the other questions – 'where do we want to be' may now be about avoiding such a crisis in future!

Third, that our own choice of response in Activity 4.4 reveals something about our own predilections for leadership work. Keep in mind, this simple tool is really about responding to change; how are we in our minds doing that? If we conflate the five questions to six (because the Checking question has two components), we can see a pattern emerging.

Visioning – where do we want to be?   1

Planning – how will we get there?

Facilitating – what resources are necessary?   2

Doing – what actions happen?

Checking 1 – what results have we achieved   3

Checking 2 – where are we now?

Activity 4.5

What is the pattern emerging when we consider the six questions in three groups of two questions, as outlined above? What do Visioning and Planning have in common? What do Facilitating and Doing have in common? What do the two Checking questions have in common? One familiar concept connects and differentiates them.

The connecting and *revealing* idea is time: vision/planning are both future orientated; whereas facilitating/doing are present orientated; and checking, which is essentially evaluating what has been done, is past orientation. It should not surprise us, then, that a genuine change tool has

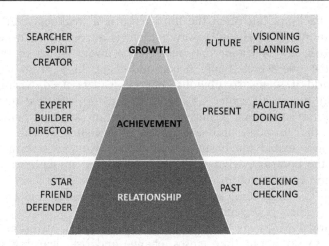

Figure 4.5 Time and the Five Elements

time tenses built into it when we examine its structure. Figure 4.5 shows the tenses and also aligns them with the motivators and Relationship-Achievement-Growth type motivators (RAG). But to pick up the earlier point about own predilections: some leaders have a future orientation, some a present, and some a past. Which were you when you answered the vacation question of Activity 4.4? Projecting where you wanted to be? Excited by what you might be doing? Or re-experiencing what happened before?

There is no right or wrong here, or better or worse even. People – leaders – usually have one strong predilection (for Future, Present, Past) with a good

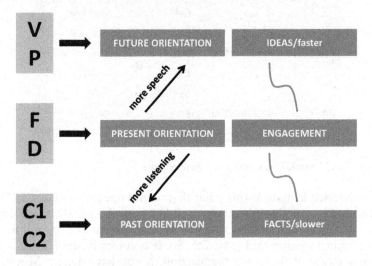

Figure 4.6 Characteristics of The Five Elements Model

secondary back-up; but often the third tense is a weakness that threatens to prove an Achilles' Heel. However, there is a context in which we all have to work, and a leader may need to be aware which of these three tenses is the one which really needs addressing in a given context. In today's world it seems so obvious that all leaders need 'vision' (future orientation) and so all leader CVs seem to lard up with that quality (certainly at interview!); but it may well be that in a given context – for example – the visionary and fast-growth of a company whose founding CEO has now exited the business that more 'vision' is not the essential need. On the contrary, what such an organisation might need might be consolidation (present tense), or even, if the original CEO has almost gone too far, too fast, that some serious Checking (past tense) is in order before going any further. It depends.[11]

Motivational Maps, as we know, not only tracks motivation, but also has plenty to say about time tenses, change and risk, learning styles and more besides.[12] So here, too, we find the three aspects of The Five Elements Model have further properties, and these may well remind us of the Maps.

Thinking about tenses – past, present and future – is a useful way of considering all and any change. So this tool is a useful complement to the Motivational Maps.

To remind ourselves about time in the Maps[13]:

TENSE	MOTIVATORS		5 ELEMENTS	SHARED PROPERTIES
FUTURE	GROWTH	Se	V	Ideas
		Sp	P	Faster
		Cr		Supremacy
PRESENT	ACHIEVEMENT	Ex	F	Things
		Bu	D	Medium Speed
		Di		Utility
PAST	RELATIONSHIP	St	C1	Facts
		Fr		Slower
		De	C2	Quality

Figure 4.7 Time, Tenses, Maps, and The Five Elements

It is important to state at this point that we are not saying that C1/C2, D/F, P/V are always exactly equivalent to RAG, but the parallels are clear. A future orientation will tend to result in G-type motivators, as well as a tendency to want to vision and plan, etc. So, it becomes incumbent on a leader to become aware of their own predilection. If you have done a Motivational

Map, you will know which of the three RAG elements most dominates your energy (or, if it mixed). Now ask yourself this:

Activity 4.6

Leave aside your motivational profile temporarily, and consider: are you somebody who typically likes to imagine future possibilities, and/or likes to plan what is going to happen? Or do you prefer making things happen by managing and facilitating? Finally, or do you like to check and make sure you have done what you said you'd do or you have taken stock of exactly what your position is now? Indeed, if you had to rank order these three mind states, which is the most and which the least important to you (see Figure 4.8)? Whereas motivational profiles can be truly mixed, we find that this is not so much the case with The Five Elements Model.

Given your result, you should now understand that this is your strength, alongside your secondary strength too; but that your third element is something that needs careful watching as a leader because potentially it could undermine all your achievements: through oversight, which is to say that no project is ever fully completed, and so is weakened; through assumption, which is to say that we recruit and treat others as if they shared our predilections, thus creating conformity, through over-reliance on one element or two, which involves their overuse and eventual impairment. On this last point, we have all come across the new leader who simply spins out vision, vision, vision to their teams; initially, this energises, but finally it tires if there is nothing more than a vision. At the other end of the spectrum, we have also met the leader who continually checks the data, confirms the facts, requires more research, and ultimately is so risk-averse their group never move forward, and they fail because they never really launched!

So, let us now look in a little more detail at the areas involved in The Five Elements Model.

Notice now we divide the 'Checking' questions in the middle at the checkpoint in order to arrive at a familiar sequence in business planning:[14] starting with 'where are we now?' and ending with 'what results have we achieved?' In this way the Checking element or modality acts like two bookends to protect,

5 ELEMENTS	TENSE	RANK ORDER 1st, 2nd or 3rd
VP	FUTURE	
FD	PRESENT	
C1 C2	PAST	

Figure 4.8 Rank order of the Five Elements

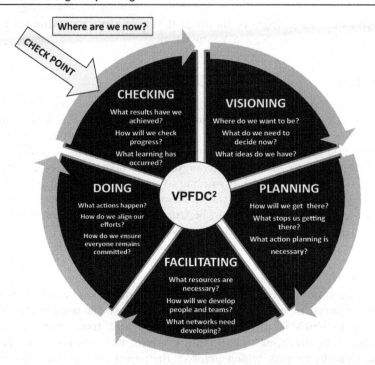

Figure 4.9 The Five Elements cycle

as it were, the whole process. The assumption would normally be that before we vision we need a reality check on where we are; and that once we have delivered the actions, then we need to review or evaluate how we actually did – before asking again, where are we now?

Beside the main questions that each of The Five Elements demands of us, there are two subsidiary questions that help us enlarge upon each of its issues. If we take the widest possible question from an organisational point of view, these questions may look this:

1 C1: Where is our organisation now?

   Financially and with marketing/sales?
   Operationally and with our employees?

2 V: Where do we want our organisation to be?

   So, what decisions do we need to make now?
   What ideas do we have?

3 P: How will we get there?

   What stops us getting there?

What action planning is necessary?

4   F: What resources are necessary?

How will we develop people and teams?
What networks need developing?

5   D: What actions happen?

How do we align our efforts?
How do we ensure everyone remains committed?

6   C2: What results have we achieved?

How will we check progress?
What learning has occurred?

Activity 4.7

Consider your own organisation. There are 6 primary questions and 12 secondary questions. Whether you own your business, whether you are a senior level executive, or whether you are an employee, think about these questions and put yourself in the shoes of being a leader, even if you are not. How would you respond to them? Can you answer them? What issues arise as a result of taking them on board? Which question causes you the most 'pain' or produces the most issues?[15]

The Five Elements tool has many threads that we will not be covering in this chapter or book, but we will be returning to it in a lot more detail in two subsequent volumes in this series.[16] But from the leadership perspective now there are two things that we are trying to emphasise. First, which we have partially done, to emphasise the need to a leader to have a planning tool, an heuristic device,[17] that enables them to look at any challenge and provide a framework – at least a preliminary one – on which to hang, analyse and ultimately solve the problem(s). In short, helping the leader think about and plan what they need to do.

But second, there is also another aspect of this tool that we need to notice now and think through its implications. Just as we have noted that the five elements actually divide into the three time tenses, so there is another important distinction to make between V, P, F, D and C2. So here is the answer: F and D are qualitatively different from V, P and C2.

Activity 4.8

Take another look at the six Primary questions relating to VPFDC2 in Figure 4.9. In what significant way is F and D different from the other questions? Indeed, in another sense, why – in our opinion – are these the two most difficult questions to answer, at least for most leaders?

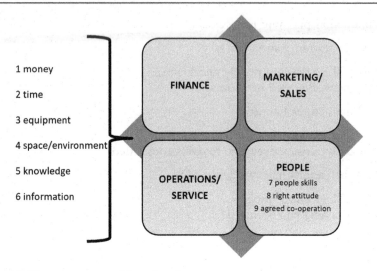

1 money

2 time

3 equipment

4 space/environment

5 knowledge

6 information

FINANCE

MARKETING/
SALES

OPERATIONS/
SERVICE

PEOPLE
7 people skills
8 right attitude
9 agreed co-operation

Figure 4.10 Nine resources and four domains

The answer to the question in this activity is simply this: people! When we are Visioning and Planning, then we are in our heads, thinking about the future; when we are Checking, essentially reviewing the quality of what we have done or considering exactly where we are as a result of past inputs, then we too are thinking about our results. But when we are resourcing or facilitating (F) or what is to happen (at D for Doing), then we are having to interact with our employees or our people in the present in order to engage them in delivering the plan; furthermore, once we get facilitation underway, we have the ongoing issue of sustaining the momentum – through the people. This comes back to a theme running through all our Mapping Motivation books: namely, the difficulty of dealing with people which is essentially to do with dealing with ambiguity and uncertainty. And we know that dealing with ambiguity is something most leaders – that is, those who have the 'position' of leader within an organisation – most want to avoid.[18] In truth, we all prefer to work with certainties, but it is the special task of the true leader to cut through the certainties and embrace ambiguity. Why? Because "Change projects are ambiguous," as Krause observed. This has been recognised for a long, long time, though it continually needs to be re-stated; again, Krause[19] writing on the leadership philosophy of Sun Tzu comments, "It is particularly difficult to be flexible when resources are limited. To do so requires subjective ability – tolerance of ambiguity – of a very high order". Leaders, then, who marshal resources effectively must, by definition, be masters in handling ambiguity; and the ambiguity is most acute when leading people or dealing with people in any other capacity – for example as customer or supplier.

Let's consider, then, some further aspect of F and D and dig a little more deeply. F asks:

What resources are necessary?
How will we develop people and teams?
What networks need developing?

These are big, broad-brush questions. But we know from our first volume[20] that there are nine types of resources and four key organisational areas in which they apply.

If we look at Figure 4.10 we see that six of the Resources are listed down the left hand side. The arrow indicates that they could go into any of the four Domains of Finance, Marketing/Sale, Operations/Service and People, although typically 'money' is a resource in the Finance domain and from there it spreads out to feed the other three: so, for example, money may purchase the technology/equipment that may be needed in the Operations/Service area. But knowledge and information are almost certainly required in all domains: we need timely information on cash flow in Finance, or we need sensitive information about the market or our prospects in Marketing/Sale, or we need information about new technology for our operations; and of course we certainly need information about our people in the People domain: what motivates them, are they engaged, what are their current concerns, and so on.

But we see that three questions are really very specifically just about the People: do we have the people skills we need, do staff have the right attitudes (and motivation) and are we able to agree to co-operate? Put another way, that last question means: have we got functioning teams, as opposed to mere groups working in silos? We will be looking at this in Chapter 6 (the F of the model). In Chapter 5 we will be studying the how to get things done (the D of the model). But for now let us return to the thinking strategically.

Activity 4.9

The six questions (in Figure 4.11) need to operate in all four domains of organisational or business life. Consider them, therefore, across the finance/marketing and sales/ operations and services/ people of your organisation. What, when you do this, emerges as the number 1 issue for you? Notice whether an issue in one domain has a knock-on effect in another. For example, cash flow or sales revenue may be the most pressing and immediate concern; but if so, what is the marketing strategy and is the sales process aligned with it? Or, even supposing it were, what of the quality or price of the product in the market place? Or what of the employees, and the quality of the customer service, speed of response to complaints, for example? In other words, try to find, first, where there is the biggest problem, and then second, where there are connections between them. Third, of course, having established what the situation

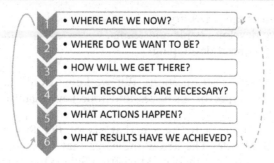

WHAT IS YOUR NUMBER 1 PRIORITY ISSUE?

Figure 4.11 Six key questions across the four domains

actually is, then one can prioritise as to where the work needs to be done to improve the situation.

And remember, this tool is iterative, which means that having 'scoped' the whole organisation in this way, and having identified, for example, lack of sales revenues as the most pressing problem, then use the tool again on the sales revenue issue. We have established in the initial sweep where we are with the sales revenue – somewhere not good, somewhere perhaps where if this continues we will go bankrupt in six months – but now: where do we want to be? And how will we ...? And so on.

When we come to thinking about the future, the leader will need to take on board all the factors: mission, values, vision, reality checks and more beside. But ultimately, the leader is going to have to set goals as the primary mechanism for setting direction and also for aligning staff with purpose. And in setting goals, which are congruent with mission, vision, and values, the leader must ensure that they – and the senior team – are not just talking, but doing too. Doing is the focus of our next chapter.

Notes

1 We obviously advocate Motivational Maps as the tool of choice here, but recognise that other tools can provide a 'language' in which issues of performance and efficiency (if not specifically motivation) can be discussed. Perhaps the most well-known would be the Belbin Inventory which identifies team roles: https://bit.ly/2Bb9XEa.

2 For more on this see *Mapping Motivation*, James Sale, Routledge (2016), page 71. Essentially, the 80:20 Rule implies a 4:1 distribution of results. This means there are four levels of motivation/performance – plus one (+). The extra level is not counted as a fifth level because it is a 0 – no motivation at all, no performance at all.

3 And as a reminder: we do not class self-awareness or self-development as a skill, but more as a quality that one possesses (or not). Also, in *Mapping Motivation* when we refer to 'skills' we usually mean and include the

'knowledge' too that is required to be undertake some specific work or job successfully.

4 Indeed, according to Brian Tracy, every two or three months a problem presents itself to an organisation which potentially, if not handled properly, will sabotage or sink the organisation. *Breaking the Success Barriers*, Nightingale Conant (2014).

5 Burnout most obviously leads to the well-known phenomenon of absenteeism, which is well studied in management literature. But it also leads to 'presenteeism' which is less well appreciated, though more directly correlated with disengagement at work. Wikipedia defines presenteeism this way: "Presenteeism or working while sick can cause productivity loss, poor health, exhaustion and workplace epidemics. While the contrasting subject of absenteeism has historically received extensive attention in the management sciences, presenteeism has only recently been studied. Certain occupations such as welfare and teaching are more prone to presenteeism. Doctors may attend work while sick due to feelings of being irreplaceable. Jobs with large workloads are associated with presenteeism. People whose self-esteem is based on performance, as well as workaholics, typically have high levels of presenteeism. Presenteeism may have many motives. An employee may come to work because they simply need the money and cannot afford to take time off due to illness. Additionally, one could go to work due to a love and devotion to the job. In this case, presenteeism could be considered an act of organizational citizenship and inspire admiration from colleagues. Other reasons include feeling that their career prospects may be damaged if they take time off, and an expectation of presence driven from management" – https://bit.ly/2DVbNvc.

6 James Sale and Steve Jones, *Mapping Motivation for Engagement*, Routledge (2019), Chapter 7.

7 We call it The Five Elements Model because it is analogous to the famous '5 Elements' of Chinese medicine and the cycle they go through: Wood, Fire, Earth, Metal, and Water. In this sequence all things change and become something else: fire destroys wood and transmutes it to ash (earth) and from the earth metal is mined, and on metal water condenses, and then from water the plant (wood) grows. The importance of the sequence lays in its interconnectedness, and in the fact that all are necessary to achieve completion. Indeed, the Chinese model is attuned to various other factors, and most especially the seasons: wood (Spring – growth, vitality), fire (Summer – flowering, energised), earth (late Summer – levelling, fruition), metal (Autumn – harvesting, collecting) and water (Winter – retreat, stillness). See Wikipedia – https://bit.ly/2B5KScc. For a detailed account of this as a healing modality see: Carola Beresford-Cooke, Shiatsu: Theory and Practice, Elsevier, (1996/2003). Also, there are many versions of this kind of five-step process around in management. A useful parallel to our model is a digital model from Joe Dettman, Adam Canwell and Richard Wellins in their Digital-Era Leadership cycle from their 'Key digital-era Leadership Capabilities' article. This has, like ours, five steps: Drive, Navigate, Connect, Relate and Think. See https://bit.ly/2EUH6nA.

8 We take the view that those who do not plan, plan to fail. "Small business survival rates are as high as 91 per cent after one year of trading, but after five years just four in ten small businesses will still be trading, research finds" – https://bit.ly/2RZzOWG. Obviously, planning is just one aspect of failure, but this particular article stresses weak cash flow as a significant cause, but ensuring the receipt of revenues is surely a planning issue to begin with.

9 As Dwight D Eisenhower observed: "...Plans are worthless, but planning is everything. [...] it is unexpected, therefore it is not going to happen the way you are planning. [...] But if you haven't been planning you can't start to work, intelligently at least. That is the reason it is so important to plan, to keep yourselves steeped in the character of the problem that you may one day be called upon to solve..." – extract from: 'Remarks at the National Defense Executive Reserve Conference', 14 November 1957.

10 Whether academic treatises can be equated with corporate plans may also be debated, but there is a dangerous tendency at all levels for planning to become a static plan. According to one text, for example, a corporate plan should include the following: Introduction, Assumptions, Primary Objectives, Secondary Objectives, Strengths and Weaknesses, Statement of Expected Results, Risk and Sensitivity, Strategies, Operational Improvements, Organisation and Management, Diversification, Finance, Contingency Plan, Criteria for Effective Planning, and Timescales. Quite a lot of text, then! From *Check it – Do it! Checklists for Business*, William Shaw and Graham Day, Century Business, Random House (1995).

11 And it should be obvious from the earlier connection that we have made with the Chinese five Elements, which are 'seasonal', that 'it depends' means it depends where on the cycle where we are; and also that this is a cycle, which means all things come round in their term. We cannot get fixated on one element and think that it can solve all our problems, all of the time.

12 Seeing *Mapping Motivation*, ibid.

13 See *Mapping Motivation for Coaching*, James Sale and Bevis Moynan, Routledge (2018) Chapter 5.

14 Actually, we talk about the familiar sequences, but sometimes such sequences are not all that familiar: there seems to be hundreds of versions of how to write a business plan. There is a world of difference between writing the plan and planning – that gerund again. We are not interested in providing instructions on how to write a plan, but more on the actual planning steps themselves. In other words, what does the leader need to think about and do. To get a sense of how different business plan advice might be from what we are advocating (which is not to be critical), consider Growthink's recommendation and five-step process: the business plan process includes Research, Strategize, Calculate, Draft, Revise and Proofread (https://bit.ly/2O4kvsz). Clearly, there are good reasons for doing these five things, but we prefer our own model, and the idea that one is always revising the plan anyway rather than getting it 'right'.

15 This tool clearly has personal development applications too, as our initial query regarding vacations implied; and so these questions can be used as an extension of the work we covered in Chapter 2. Having completed the organisational perspective, re-consider these same questions from a personal point of view. Of course, in doing it personally you will substitute all plurals for singular pronouns: 'Where is our organisation now?' becomes 'Where am I now?' and so on. Again, a key answer to focus on is the one which causes you the most problems to answer effectively or satisfactorily. These questions parallel the more typical life map questions: Who am I? Where have I come from? Where am I going? What is stopping me? How will I get there? What help do I need? What will it be like when I get there? – from *The Personal Management Handbook*, John Mulligan, Marshall Editions (1988).

16 The use of The Five Elements tool in team building will be dealt with more fully in *Mapping Motivation for Top Performing Teams*, Routledge (2020), and its use in *Mapping Motivation for Innovation, Strategy and Change*, Routledge (2021).

17 According to Encyclopedia.com an "Heuristic device is any procedure which involves the use of an artificial construct to assist in the exploration of social phenomena. It usually involves assumptions derived from extant empirical research. For example, ideal types have been used as a way of setting out the defining characteristics of a social phenomenon, so that its salient features might be stated as clearly and explicitly as possible. A heuristic device is, then, a form of preliminary analysis. Such devices have proved especially useful in studies of social change, by defining benchmarks, around which variation and differences can then be situated. In this context, a heuristic device is usually employed for analytical clarity, although it can also have explanatory value as a model" – https://bit.ly/2ACEWcB. Organisations and businesses are of course 'social phenomenon'.

18 For more on our reasoning and ideas on this see, *Mapping Motivation*, ibid., Chapter 1.

19 *The Way of the Leader*, Donald G Krause, Nicolas Brealey (1997). Sun Tzu wrote *The Art of War* some 2,500 years ago.

20 *Mapping Motivation*, ibid.

Chapter 5

Leaders doing

You may have noticed by now an overlap between two models that we are proposing for leaders to adopt. The first model, our actual leadership model, is the '4+1' model which helps us understand both the key areas where leaders must function and the areas where they need to develop four key skill sets, and at the same time commit to personal development at a profound level. Notice that these five items on the list are all discrete; they are separate qualities/skills we need to do and to develop. On the other hand, 'The Five Elements' model is an interactive, heuristic device to help leaders solve problems. The items, therefore, are not discrete, but interlinked, and to only focus on one, and ignore the others, is a sure way to lead one's organisation into serious trouble. But when we set them out, side by side, we see that there are important overlaps, although not an exact fit.

Activity 5.1

What do you notice about this schematic comparison shown in Figure 5.1? What, perhaps, is the single most important observation that we might make from a leadership perspective?

In our view what is important to grasp is that one way or another being a leader means working with and positively influencing people. Starting with oneself, and asking, 'where am I now?' and seeking to develop one's self-awareness, understanding and capabilities as we have demonstrated in Chapter 2 and 3. Then, we need to mobilise others: individually, team-wise and at an organisational level. All the strategy and vision in the world are not going to go anywhere unless we can Do, Build Teams and Motivate or, to use The Five Elements Model, unless we can Facilitate and Do. At a rough estimate, then, looking at Figure 5.1, one might say that 70–80% of leadership is really about developing, motivating and empowering people to perform. Of course, that doesn't mean the 20–30% of leadership left for Thinking and Strategy is small beer; as the Pareto Principle makes clear, small things can be vital things: The Thinking and the Doing need to be interlocked, but the critical thing is realising that the Doing is not simply action (though that too); it

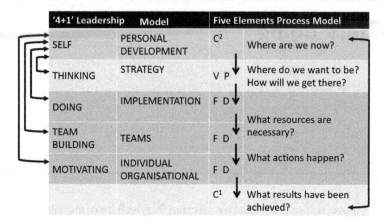

'4+1' Leadership	Model	Five Elements Process Model	
SELF	PERSONAL DEVELOPMENT	C²	Where are we now?
THINKING	STRATEGY	V P	Where do we want to be? How will we get there?
DOING	IMPLEMENTATION	F D	
TEAM BUILDING	TEAMS	F D	What resources are necessary?
MOTIVATING	INDIVIDUAL ORGANISATIONAL	F D	What actions happen?
		C¹	What results have been achieved?

Figure 5.1 Comparing Leadership '4+1' and The Five Elements Models

is specifically action that activates others, our staff, our employees, and all stakeholders for that matter.

Clearly, in a book of this nature, we are not covering the full sweep of all the things that leaders need to address. What we want to look at is how motivation and Motivational Maps play their part in this drama that faces all leaders. If we consider what they need to 'do', then, clearly there are some 'things' they do which do not require a motivational understanding; we leave the bulk of those other 'things' for other books!

Activity 5.2

What major activities/skills would you consider not motivationally driven, and yet which leaders need to have?

The kind of things we are thinking of here are the need for leaders to be good at things like: goal-setting, time management, leading or chairing meetings, systematising processes, creating turn-key operations, and so on. It may be argued, taking time management as one example, that freeing up more time is motivational for an individual, or – to take another example – that chairing a meeting well also involves motivational skills. We would accept that, but in so far these activities require more intellectual skills and compartmentalisation, then they are not the same as, or full-on, as the issue of people development. We'll get to the 'full-on' people development via teams in Chapters 6 and 7, and on an individual basis in Chapter 8, but for now let's consider the overlap of the '4+1' Model, that requires Doing, and The Five Elements heuristic model which also has an element called 'Doing'. What would the 'doing' in the '4+1' model look like if we applied the problem-solving technique of The Five Elements to it? Keep in mind, as we said The Five Elements is iterative: we can apply it to the biggest 'big picture', or use it to focus on some small or even very small component of what we are attempting to achieve.

Let's break down what the leader has to do at each stage of The Five Elements process, and ask the questions, and thus provide a handy checklist of activities: of 'doings'!

If we start with Checking, then we already know from Chapter 4 that the four key questions to address are: what results have we achieved? How will we check progress? What learning has occurred? Where is our organisation now – financially / marketing / sales / operationally / and with employees? These are good overarching questions but to drill down a bit further we might consider the following in Figure 5.2.

For more on the nine Resources go to Figure 4.10 And on the final evaluative question, do not forget what we discussed in Chapter 1 on the association of leadership with play/fun: play/fun massively enhances the 'quality of experience' for nearly all employees.

Activity 5.3

Between Monitor and Evaluate there are eight sub-heading questions in Figure 5.2. Even if you are a leader of one person – just yourself – go through these questions and answer them for your current work or projects. Rate, too,

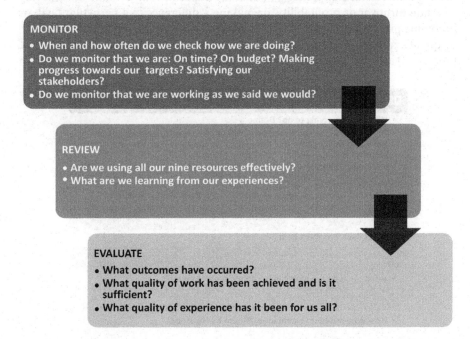

Figure 5.2 The big check

how good or effective you think your answers are. So, for example, if you check how you are doing once a year on the 31 December, is that good enough? How would you score yourself out of 10? Think, what would really be ideal as answers for each of these questions. Which two or three scores are lowest? These provide a focus for the next stage, Visioning.

It should be clear that a central feature of the these checking questions is that they provide a leader with a detailed analysis of any situation. In Chapter 4 we considered in Figure 4.8 where you, as a leader, considered your natural strengths to be in terms of Future, Present and Past orientation. We commented that many leaders are very future-orientated, which in some ways is good and necessary, but the Achilles' Heel can be just this failure to Check where we are and what we have achieved. If the leader is not expert at this element, then finding someone who is and delegating is essential.

The Vision questions from Chapter 4 are: where do we want our organisation to be? So, what decisions do we need to make now? And, what ideas do we have? Let's expand these further.

To add a little more explanation to Figure 5.3, consider: the vision question becomes the simple and homely inquiry – what are we trying to do? Over the next three–five years? Sometimes when we talk about 'vision' or 'THE Vision' to staff,[1] their eyes glaze over; it sounds sometimes too much like a big abstraction. But, what are we trying to do? Everyone can understand that. It can range from beating a successful competitor(s), obtaining a specific market share or achieving a certain turnover or profitability, or making a difference in a particular field, or becoming pre-eminent in a certain domain, or developing a reputation for results or quality, and so on. One thing, however, is sure: most people prefer, and are more motivated by, a genuine vision that makes a difference to others rather than

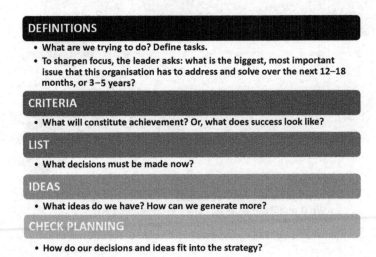

Figure 5.3 Expanding the Vision

the mere pursuit of money and profit.[2] Clarity is everything; so, what tasks need to be done to get to realising the vision? List these tasks. And, what will constitute achievement or what does success really look like? One here should be able to see, hear and be able to touch what success feels like in one's imagination; in this way it becomes a reality to the sub-conscious mind, and so a compelling driving force. Leaders understand that all achievement originally stems from desire – strong, intense, compelling desire – and desire is fuelled by the images the imagination (and dreams too) creates.

Finally, given that one can see and feel this big picture and has broken it down into specific tasks, then what decisions need to be made and in what order? Imagine you are going to make a cake, because you like cake: what ideas do you have to make it as delicious as possible? How can you enrich the final product that is the cake? You can bake an ordinary cake, but you want more than that? How can you get more ideas on making this as fabulous as possible?[3]

Activity 5.4

If you are a leader, expand your vision by running your current vision through the sieve of the questions in Figure 5.3. If you are not a leader, then use the same questions from a personal standpoint – in other words, consider your life as requiring a vision. Thus, starting with Definitions, simply change the wording to 'What am I trying to do (over the next three–five years)?' and so on with the other questions. Note what is clear to you about the future you want, and what is less clear and requires further work. We tend to find, both for leaders in organisations and individuals imagining their futures, that there is a common shortfall: namely, that we can all project big visions that sound grand, but what's involved

STRATEGIES
- How are going to achieve our goals?
- How clear is everybody about how we are doing this?
- To sharpen focus, the leader asks: what one thing, if we did it, is most likely to enable us to succeed?

FEASIBILITY
- How feasible are these proposals?
- What problems can we foresee?
- To sharpen focus, the leader asks: what is the biggest single obstacle preventing achievement of our goals?
- Double check our Facilitating (F), especially for the nine Resources

SCHEDULE
- See Figure 5.5

Figure 5.4 Planning priorities

Who specifically will be doing what exactly, and when will they do it, and where will they be?			
WHO?	WHAT?	WHEN?	WHERE?

Figure 5.5 Action plan schedule

(the tasks) are less clear, and even murkier are the decisions to be made, and most startlingly, there is often a complete lack of exciting, new ideas.

But if you do this appropriately you will realise exactly what we said before: namely, that The Five Elements hang together. For the final question – how do our decisions and ideas fit into the strategy? – obviously leads on to integrating the big picture into a manageable plan, or Planning.

Questions already established for Planning are: How will we get there? What stops us getting there? What action planning is necessary? Let's add some further depth to these points (see Figure 5.4 and Figure 5.5).

We have got to the point now where the bones of our visioning is beginning to take on flesh and blood, as action planning starts setting out what needs to be done. Before moving on, however, to the Facilitating (F), let's review the 'focus' questions in V and P in Figure 5.6:

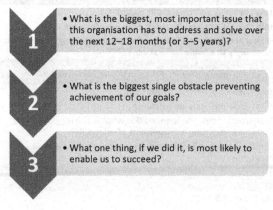

1
• What is the biggest, most important issue that this organisation has to address and solve over the next 12–18 months (or 3–5 years)?

2
• What is the biggest single obstacle preventing achievement of our goals?

3
• What one thing, if we did it, is most likely to enable us to succeed?

Figure 5.6 Three priority or focus questions for any leader

These three questions do concentrate the mind wonderfully; they are really aspects of two important ideas: one, the entrepreneur mind-set,[4] which effective leaders have, and two, which in turn derives from 80–20 thinking.[5] 80/20 thinking always asks us to consider the vital few amidst the trivial many; so these questions take that idea to its logical conclusion – *one* thing to consider is the fewest![6] Which issue is most important; which *one* obstacle is our biggest barrier to success; which *one* thing, if we did that, would make a difference?

Activity 5.5

Consider the three questions in Figure 5.6, either as a leader within an organisation, or in terms of your personal life (so, if the latter, what is the biggest, most important issue you have to address over the next 12–18 months, and so on). As a leader, what possible issues arise from these questions?

From our experience working in this field, we find the following issues typical. For question 1, a lack of a common mission or of shared objectives; a lack of consensual values resulting in conflict; a lack of teamwork and how to work as a team; and finally, and critically, a lack of, or failure in, communications, be that in systems or with people, and in the latter case a sense of individual isolation. Apart from the first point, lack of common mission,[7] these are all people-related problems for the leadership.[8]

For question 2, we find five major issues: obstacles caused by lack of knowledge or skills; by wrong and inappropriate attitudes; by lack of leadership development; by lack of customer focus; and by having the wrong people in the wrong jobs! Again, we see that the primary blocks tend to be people-related issues for the leadership, and even that the leaders themselves need new and better development.

Finally, for question 3, we find seven major steps that really tend to make a big difference in outcomes: clarifying the mission, the vision and/or the goals; ensuring there is teamwork and creating a team agreement (which we cover in Chapter 6); reviewing how the senior team interacts within its self; appointing or promoting new blood; developing a more systems approach to people;[9] upskilling at all levels, but especially at management level, and particularly including planning, delegating and motivating skills; and adopting a change management approach to organisational development – which means, if we start at the beginning – identifying and promoting core values, or becoming clear about what we stand for. Notice here that the first and last points are similar in that they require clarification: clarification of mission/vision and clarification of our values. What this typically leads to is all our ducks in a row, or what might more technically be called alignment. We cannot do everything at once, but if we can change one significant thing, then we look for other aspects of our work to more readily be aligned as well.

It should be clear from all this that leadership and developing people is where all great achievement is to be found. If we now look at Facilitating, which is tantamount to resourcing tangibles, intangibles and people, then what might this look like? We have in Figure 4.9 identified three questions already: what resources are necessary? How will we develop people and teams? What networks need developing? Let's expand on this.

Activity 5.6

Go through the list in Figure 5.7 and ask yourself how successfully, out of 10, are we doing each of these items. 'Do we have enough money?' may not just be a yes or no answer; for if 'no', then 9/10 might mean we are very close to the sum required, whereas 2/10 might be mean we are so far short as to seem unbridgeable with our current ideas and strategy. 10/10 would mean we do have the required amount. Each answer should generate further insights into what is next for the leadership.

We are asking in Figure 5.7 (and elsewhere) very simple questions, and we think this is important; but when these questions are unpacked they become fully topical and relevant. By which we mean, they tie into well-defined areas of management interest and concern. Take our last question: are we successfully persuading people to work with us? This question has wide ramifications: people working 'with us' includes suppliers and other stakeholders; it touches, too, on how our brand is perceived in the marketplace, so whether customers or clients will want to engage with us and our products or services. But most critically of all, this is about employees. As Sir Richard Branson put it: 'Clients do not come first. Employees come first. If you take care of your employees, they will take care of the clients'.[10] So, what we are talking about

ISSUES
- Do we have the necessary resources?
- Tangibles: Money, Equipment, Space/Environment
- Intangibles: Time, Knowledge, Information
- People Development: People Skills, Attitude, Agreed Co-operation

ENCOURAGEMENT
- Are we encouraging each other?
- Are we promoting ourselves to those who benefit from our work?

NEGOTIATION
- Are we successfully persuading people to work with us?

Figure 5.7 Facilitating the action

here is, first, recruitment and getting the very best people into your organisation; and second, retention – holding onto them so that they don't want to leave. Two core skills, then, of the leader is the ability to recruit effectively, and to reward and retain the best employees. In Chapter 7 we will return to the topic of recruitment[11] in the difficult sense of how do Maps help us when we have recruited the wrong leader for the role?

We come, then, to action, the Doing. So far as leadership is concerned, and possibly so far as everyone is concerned, this is the most important element of leadership. It is action-orientation that marks out the leader; constant, continual and consistent action. Without action all the thinking in the world is ineffectual. Again, to quote Sir Richard Branson, a world-famous leader, noted for his success, especially with people: "A good leader doesn't get stuck behind a desk".[12] And to put this another way, leaders have an "unwavering resolve … to do what must be done".[13]

The Doing is arguably the most important element of The Five Elements Model (although we have stressed the essential and interconnected nature of all five components), for without the Doing all is futile. Why have a vision, or why bother checking its accomplishment, if nothing is done or going to be done? And here are two very important psychological observations:[14] first, according to Jung, "There can be no transforming…of apathy into movement without emotion". Second, according to Donald Calne, "The essential difference between emotion and reason is that emotion leads to action while reason leads to conclusions". At the heart of the action that the leader must initiate there is the striking realisation that action is emotional, not intellectual or merely cognitive. Emotions drive energy, and as we know, energy is motivation.

In Figure 4.9 we identified three questions that characterise effective action: what actions happen? How do we align our efforts? How do we ensure everyone remains committed? Let's expand these questions further in Figure 5.8.

A few remarks to help elucidate these 10 questions.

Question 5 of Figure 5.8 refers to 'sides', an odd word in this context; what do we mean by it? Anyone who has worked in any organisation of any size will know that as well as getting the job done, and achieving targets, there is also the matter of internal politics, fiefdoms and empire building. Where there is effective management, this is minimised. But what we are referring to here is the way that different departments, groupings, teams, faculties (or however we nominate them) tend to operate without reference to either other departments (i.e. 'sides') or even the whole organisation. So, for example, we might find that the finance department and the operations go their own separate ways, or that marketing and sales never communicate, because that's not their 'job'. And this extends vertically too: that senior or middle management start forming a caste, club or 'in-group' that excludes others from real-time information and access to resources. We sometimes call this a 'silo mentality'.[15] It is the job of the leader to spot this, if it starts to happen or is happening, and

COMMUNICATE – before and during the project run	
1	Are our plans turning into actions?
2	Have we made the best use of our resources?
3	Are the tasks clearly defined?
4	Is the work clearly explained to those who will contribute?
5	Does each side know what the other is doing? And, who are the 'sides'?
6	Is the workload balanced?
7	Are we using our contacts and networks to best effect?
8	Are we working together effectively as a team?
9	Is anyone becoming disaffected, disengaged, or feeling undervalued?
10	How can I help?

Figure 5.8 What we need to do

to stop it.[16] As we have already seen in Chapters 2 and 3, and are going to see especially in Chapter 6, the language of Motivational Maps can help here as part of the facilitating process.

Second, question 6, is the workload balanced? This is not just a question of fairness or parity in today's working world, which various authorities now describe as a VUCA[17] world. That is to say, not just a question of making sure the load is equitably distributed. It is now as much about wellness, and our responsibility to keep our employees healthy, physically, emotionally and mentally. The VUCA acronym derives from the American military operations in hazardous conditions in the Middle East; we now read a lot more about troops coming home and experiencing extreme health problems, often summed up in the phrase, Post-Traumatic Stress Disorder (PTSD[18]), than ever we did in the twentieth century. So too in the workplace, there has been an alarming increase in stress, anxiety, depression and general emotional and mental problems in today's commercial environment: according to the World Health Organization,[19] for example, global failure to tackle depression and anxiety is costing the world nearly $1 trillion a year in lost productivity; and further, without scaled-up treatment, there will be a staggering 12 billion working days, or 50 million years of work lost to depression and anxiety disorders between now and 2030. It puts the annual cost to the global economy at $925 billion (or £651 billion). Clearly, this is a problem on a global scale, and we are not pretending that Mapping Motivation is some sort of panacea, or a magic wand that could make all these mental issues disappear; but, we do say, as we said in the first and second volumes of this series,[20] that high levels of motivation do create and reinforce high levels of emotional resilience: when you have high motivation, you have high energy, and high energy provides a powerful immunity to anxiety, depression and even despair. Thus, as we come in the next chapter to team working and facilitation, this aspect of leadership grows ever more significant in its importance, for we are saying that the leader is there to care for the welfare of their employees at a profounder level, perhaps, than was thought appropriate in the twentieth century.

Third, questions 8 and 9 deserve mention. Once again we see the importance of team work, which is the focus of our next chapter. But note too, the necessity for the leader to go beyond simply implementing team programmes. The leader needs to take note, to observe, to be rather like Sherlock Holmes, noticing small details that are clues to what is going on emotionally with their staff. People often won't say what is wrong, explicitly, unless confronted with it (and many managers prefer not to confront); but they will reveal what they are thinking and feeling via their tone of voice, and more importantly still, their body language. If we want to, we can usually see if someone is engaged not long before the results of their work manifest themselves.

Finally, the last question, question 10, is so blindingly obvious it scarcely seems worth mentioning. But because it is obvious, it is so often overlooked. It is the job of the leader to be constantly saying to employees: how can I help? First, and where this is not officious and insincere, it is motivating for employees to have a leader who is, as it were, shoulder to the wheel with them (it also, of course, fits in with point 2 in Figure 5.8). The leader is working too; the leader is walking the talk. And, of course, as Jay Abraham[21] observed: "People are silently begging to be led". The leader's offer of help is reassuring in two ways: it implies people are doing the right thing in what they are doing, which is an encouragement to do more of it, but also that there are more resources available: at the end of the day it is the leader who can unlock these. And these possibly include: more of any of the resources we list in Figure 5.7 (and Figure 4.10). Of particular interest here is the ability of leaders, who may be strapped for more cash or time, but who can readily supply more knowledge or information, more skills expertise through coaching or mentoring, and perhaps very critically, can often get the agreed co-operation of some third party that will smooth delivery of operations for the staff. The ability of the leader to do some of these things should never be underestimated and leaders should be on the look-out to do them.

Activity 5.7

Now consider the 10 questions in Figure 5.8 and work through them. Some are open questions and some are closed,[22] but the Pareto Principle[23] will predict that two or three of the questions will prove especially hard for you to answer (or easy to answer, but the answer is not one that is satisfactory). Write down those two or three questions and your current answers to them. What action plan do you have to address these 'difficult' questions more adequately in future? Create that action plan and then – since we are in the Doing section – commit to action and – no matter how small – take the first step towards achieving it.

Having now completed the Doing, we arrive at where we started: Checking, and the key question (Figure 5.1) now to re-visit is: what results have been achieved? And so, where are we now? This, then, we think is a very powerful cycle of planning for a leader to adopt. But before leaving it and moving on specifically to the facilitation (F) that is team building in Chapter 6, there is one aspect of the leader answering the call (how can I help?) that needs further comment. Namely, types of leadership power.

Leaders have power, which is one reason why many people are attracted to them; things get done when leaders are about. But what type of powers do leaders actually have? We think there are four main types of power:[24] Positional,[25] Reward, Expert[26] and Charismatic. It's not of course that one type of power is inherently superior to another; often context is crucial as to what type of power may be applied. A 'perfect' leader (and try imagining a 'perfect' person, never mind a leader!) would effortlessly be able to deploy all four types[27] as was suitable; but the reality is, most leaders have a preferred type or style or way of operating, and usually with one or two other back-up styles.

Positional Power

- comes from the title or role of the individual, and which holds them
- accountable for results. It can, negatively, be too hierarchical, traditional, top-down, command and controlling.

Reward Power

- comes from being able to reward people for their efforts, often in 'carrot or stick' ways. Negatively, its power can diminish rapidly when rewards are not perceived as valuable or relevant.

Expert Power

- comes from having advanced skills and knowledge that others either respect or defer to, and so is a source of authority and being authoritative. Negatively, over-reliance on experts can disempower others and lead to over-reliance on one or a few voices.

Charismatic Power

- comes essentially from the individual: others give you this power because of who you are, and the respect they feel for you. Negatively, this can lead to the 'cult of personality' and blind followership.

Figure 5.9 Four types of leadership power

Activity 5.8

As a leader in any context, how do you lead others? Look at Figure 5.9. Rank order which 'type' of power you most frequently use, and then rank the other three in order of usage. Indeed, ask yourself, is there any type of leadership power that you rarely if ever use? On reflection, is that a handicap or actually no problem at all? How might reflecting on these 'types' affect how you lead in future?

What is interesting now about these four types is the fact that each of them has motivational components. The exercise of power in any context always makes a difference, for it cannot help but do so. Power makes a difference when deployed, so underpinning all power types is the desire to make a difference. But then we find that each of the four types (Position, Reward,[28] Expert, Charismatic) has two of the remaining eight motivators (Defender, Friend, Star, Director, Builder, Expert, Creator, and Spirit) more closely aligned with them.

Activity 5.9

Thinking about the four types of power, which two motivators do you consider most aligned with each of the four types? Make a note and then see if you agree with our reasoning.

First, we must say that Figure 5.10 does not represent the whole story of power types and motivators. For one thing, we do not include coercive power

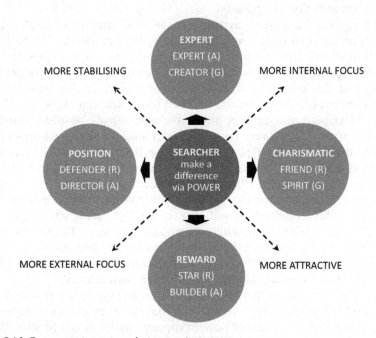

Figure 5.10 Four power types and nine motivators

here. Second, context is everything, as we like to say; so any motivator may be associated with any specific type of power. We frequently do find, for example, in the small- and medium-sized business a Managing Director (MD) who has positional power but whose number one motivator is Spirit. Keep in mind, too, that an individual usually has three motivators actively driving their actions, and these are also capable of being in conflict. But if we think about an MD who is Spirit motivator and yet holds positional power, then there is already a question about their behaviour: for independence in their actions can readily be seen by staff as an abuse of their power.

Given all that – these caveats – it does seem as if Position power most naturally aligns with the Defender and Director motivators. Why? Because Defenders like structure and hierarchy, and the Director likes to exercise power – or control; in other words, this is leadership in the organisational system, as it were. Which is an external environment. Thus, it has a stabilising effect, since it will tend (when appropriately used) to consolidate or improve the structure within which it is exercised.

Everyone can, but leaders are also ideally positioned to reward people. Rewards, typically, are external, although Motivational Maps, of course, seek in principle to redress that imbalance. But employees mainly see their rewards as: achieving recognition – sometimes leading to promotion – or, more obviously, money: a pay increase, a bonus, or commission.[29] Unlike Position power, however, this is less about creating a stable[30] structure, but more about attractive rewards that people want.

In the age we are in now, expertise is the new currency of power that is more important than ever;[31] and the desire – the motivation – to be Expert (as motivator) exactly complements this type of power. But alongside this is the allied need to innovate, which itself requires some level of expertise to be creative, and this correlates with the Creator motivator. We note that this kind of power is primarily internal – related to our learning. It is also, though the rate of change now renders any knowledge rapidly obsolete, stabilising since true expertise by its very nature provides a solid basis on which to build.

Finally, the Charismatic type of power brings together two motivators which are often considered in opposition[32] to each other: the Spirit, or maverick tendency to go it alone, and the Friend, or the desire to belong to a community. But we note that here they coincide because it is not only the more independently driven types who attract others, but also the kind of people who forge strong links with others within a community, organisation or team. The reason for this is that believing in belonging builds a sense of trust, and this is a form of attraction – we want to follow people we can trust. At the same time, Charismatic power tends to personal and internal rather than external.

The implications of all this are: without stereotyping (since an individual's motivators change over time) we may say that there are potential alignments and misalignments of the use of power types and motivational profiles. Where they coincide, as for example, Positional Power and Director motivator, we need to ask the question what, if anything, might be missing from this leader's exercise of authority? And where the type of power and the motivator(s) potentially clash, as for example, Charismatic power and Defender motivator, we need to enquire as to how that leadership functions within such inherent tensions. This is an area for leaders to explore for themselves, or better – with a Motivational Mapping coach to gain fresh insights into what they are doing, and how they can enhance their performance.

Finally, in this chapter, we return to The Five Elements' key question: what results have we achieved? And with that thought we need to come in the next chapter to more of the Facilitating and Doing that Mapping Motivation can so helpfully provide.

Notes

1 Notice that here, too, even though we are discussing 'visioning' (and subsequently 'planning'), these activities are also best done in conjunction with employees; indeed, the sharing with and communicating to staff about these elements are essential even if the leader has decided not to involve their people in inputting these domains.

2 The research on this is well summarised in Dan Pink's book, *Drive*, Canongate (2010).

3 This is such an important idea – the idea of getting new ideas! – and leaders need to get good at accessing new ideas. In Chapter 2 we used the 20 question, or Mindstorming, method for generating new ideas on improving leadership. That can be used in this situation too. But consider also – buying books by experts in this field, Edward De Bono, *Serious Creativity*, Harper Collins (1992); or Michael Gelb, *How to Think like Leonardo da Vinci*, Thorsons (1998); or a more concise book such as Geoffrey Petty, *How to be Better at Creativity*, Kogan Page (1997). Consider using your staff to generate new ideas, and especially consider those whose motivators are Creator either first or second, and where the need for ideas involves deep knowledge, look for Creator and Expert in the top three combinations; consider training courses; use a creative mentor as a sounding board, etc. Ways to improve one's creativity are virtually as endless as creativity itself. For a high-tech, modern spin on being creative at corporate level, read *Sprint: How to Solve Big Problems and Test New Ideas in Just Five Days*, by Jake Knapp, John Zeratsky, Braden Kowitz, Bantam Press (2016).

4 There are various definitions of what the entrepreneur mindset is. See, for example, Forbes, Community Voice, *6 Tips For Growing With An Entrepreneurial Mind-set*, Arash Asli, https://bit.ly/2AfeHar. This lists six aspects: Revisit Your Vision On A Daily Basis, Put Yourself In Challenging Situations, Read On A Daily Basis, Approach Problems From All Sides, Always Be In Motion, and Provide Value. This particular list doesn't mention Pareto, and why would it? But underpinning the article is the assumption of using time effectively and prioritising well – 80/20 in essence.

5 For more on 80/20 thinking see Richard Koch, *The 80/20 Principle*, Nicholas Brealey (1997); and there is a substantial amount on Motivational Maps and Pareto in James Sale and Bevis Moynan, *Mapping Motivation for Coaching*, Routledge (2018).

6 If one were to reply that zero is the fewest, we would reply that zero is not a number, and in any case if one thought that there was no issue to address, then we would deduce that one was no longer in the real world of organisational life!

98 Leaders doing

7 Even here, of course, we argue in *Mapping Motivation for Engagement*, James Sale and Steve Jones, Routledge (2018), Chapter 3, for the need for employee motivators to have a far greater impact on organisational activities than traditionally it does.

8 It is worth saying, of course, that there are other issues, for example, lack of money, and these do crop up from time to time, but the really persistent problems invariably are people ones.

9 In the UK, for example, there is the Investors in People standard – https://bit.ly/1Wf9Ewb.

10 See https://bit.ly/2DSNlLB for Branson remark.

11 See *Mapping Motivation for Engagement*, ibid., Chapter 5, for a detailed analysis of how managers may use Mapping Motivation to acquire superior candidates via the recruitment selection process.

12 See https://bit.ly/2DSNlLB.

13 Jim Collins, *From Good to Great*, Random House Business Books (2001). Collins also notes that top-level leaders are "fanatically driven, infected with an incurable need to produce results".

14 Simone Joyaux, *A Central Fact: Emotions Are the Decision-Makers* (31 August 2012), https://bit.ly/2r019eS. Joyaux cites both Jung and Calne.

15 What is 'Silo Mentality': Silo mentality is an attitude that is found in some organisations; it occurs when several departments or groups within an organisation do not want to share information or knowledge with other individuals in the same organisation. A silo mentality reduces the organisation's efficiency and can contribute to a failing corporate culture – Investopedia, https://bit.ly/2zsUOgH.

16 In Chapter 7 we look at a case where the appointed leader was in fact initiating 'silos', or 'favourites'.

17 VUCA: Volatile, Uncertain, Complex and Ambiguous. Cited by Dr Alan Watkins, *Coherence*, Kogan Page (2014) and John Knights *et al., Leading Beyond the Ego*, Routledge (2018). According to John Knights the origin of this acronym is from the American military to describe extreme conditions in Afghanistan and Iraq, but now the world more generally.

18 For a good overview, see Wikipedia: https://bit.ly/1TBD7Aq.

19 *The Lancet*. Psychiatry, Scaling-up treatment of depression and anxiety: a global return on investment analysis, D. Chisholm, *et al., The Lancet*, "Psychiatry", 12 April 2016.

20 *Mapping Motivation*, James Sale, Routledge (2016), and *Mapping Motivation for Coaching*, James Sale and Bevis Moynan, Routledge (2018).

21 "People are silently begging to be led. They are crying out to know more about a business' product or service. When you educate your customers, you'll see your profits soar" – https://bit.ly/1TBD7Aq. Jay Abraham is here referring to customers but as we already know from the Richard Branson remark, endnote 12, the employee is the number one client of the organisation!

22 Closed questions require a 'yes' or 'no' answer and tend to start with a verb such as, 'are', 'have', or 'did'; whereas open questions require more explanation and often start with 'what', 'why', or 'how'.

23 For more on the Pareto Principle, or 80/20 Rule, see *Mapping Motivation for Coaching*, ibid., Chapter 3.

24 John French and Bertram Raven, "The Bases of Social Power". D. Cartwright (Ed.), *Studies in Social Power*, Ann Arbor, MI: Institute for Social Research (1959). Also, see https://bit.ly/2zkVBCm. They identified five types of power, but we exclude 'coercive' power since it is a pathology of leadership, not an aspect we endorse or recommend. Later commentators, for example, John Prescott, https://

bit.ly/2Bz28J8 (23 August 2015) added an extra, sixth power: informational power. But we consider this, although distinctive, close enough to Expert power to be treated as one idea.

25 Positional corresponds to French and Raven's (see endnote 24) Legitimate Power, and Charismatic to their Referent Power. We think these terms are clearer, but accept others may not think so! Different authorities sometimes use different words for these types. For example, 'referent power' is sometimes referred to as 'ascribed power' – see Brian Tracy, *Victory! Applying the Proven Principles of Military Strategy to Achieve Greater Success in Your Business and Personal Life*, Tarcherperigee; Revised, Updated edition (2017).

26 Not to be confused with the Expert motivator, though the desire/motivation for expertise tends to lead to experts: people who develop advanced skills and knowledge.

27 And avoid coercion, see endnote 24, excepting of course in life and death situations where others are at risk.

28 Position power also has the ability to exercise reward power. However, we see how badly this is frequently viewed from the disengagement statistics (see *Mapping Motivation for Engagement* ibid.) and this is why Motivational Maps are crucial because it actually determines what staff want, not what the leaders in positional power think, or imagine, they want.

29 Beyond the simple and usual 'carrot and stick' (pleasure and pain) rewards, there are others – for example, training (Expert power and Expert motivator both being aligned here) – but we are considering the main reward 'play' as it were.

30 Rewards can be extremely de-stabilising since they are often contestable, and often perceived to be unfair. One of the problems of CEO leaders in the present time is the fact they often reward themselves grossly unfairly at the expense of other staff, and even shareholder returns. See David Bowles and Cary Cooper, *High Engagement*, Palgrave Macmillan (2012). In America, Bowles and Cooper cite John Mackey of Whole Foods who has capped his salary (and all executives in his company) at 19:1 to the average workers' pay. This against the corporates who increased their multiple from 47 to 81 times of the average (not lowest) earnings of staff in recent years – and yet crucially without increasing the value of their company stock. (Bowles cites evidence in the USA of 525 times greater!)

31 For the simple reason of the acceleration of change: "We're entering an age of acceleration. The models underlying society at every level, which are largely based on a linear model of change, are going to have to be redefined. Because of the explosive power of exponential growth, the 21st century will be equivalent to 20,000 years of progress at today's rate of progress; organizations have to be able to redefine themselves at a faster and faster pace". Originally published in *Perspectives on Business Innovation*. Published on KurzweilAI.net 1 May 2003 – http s://bit.ly/2Pe2GYs.

32 For more on this see *Mapping Motivation for Coaching*, ibid., Chapter 6.

Chapter 6

Leaders team building

We come now to address the fourth part of the '4+1' model: team building. As it happens, this is also a core component, although expressed in slightly different language, for The Five Elements Model or process. Leaders need to facilitate (F) and do (D), but this all hinges on getting people to work effectively for you. We will look at doing this on an individual, motivational basis in Chapter 8, but for now we wish to consider specifically the building of strong, effective teams.

In case one thought otherwise, all the research[1] and literature on good and great leadership points to the fact that team building is essential. In our first book, *Mapping Motivation*,[2] we talked about the geometric power of teams versus the arithmetic *only* strength of individuals who are not playing as a team. Initially, because developing real teams requires time and effort, a collection of talented individuals may seem to outperform a group of lesser talented individuals; but, of course, once the group actually becomes a team, then even if they are not so talented, or able, or skilled, they will still outperform the talented individuals who are merely a group. And it gets better: for if we have truly talented individuals acting as a team, then the results can be staggeringly great. Mountains can be moved, and all opposition surpassed. Let's be clear about it, Jesus Christ[3] did not change the world. He died, and according to the scriptures, he rose again – and ascended, leaving a team of 12 disciples; and those 12 disciples, that team, turned the world upside down, till finally even the pagan Roman Empire became Christian! The leader provided the lead, gave the values, mission and vision, built the team, and the team then delivered; interestingly, in this particular case, which we can regard as symbolic, the leader is not needed, is not even there,[4] as the team goes about its work. This religious example speaks of the ideal state that perhaps ought to be more prevalent in organisations: too many have leaders that may be workaholics, who either do too much or spend all their time micro-managing their subordinates. This latter case, naturally enough, disempowers and disengages employees. Either way, it does not lead to great teams.

So what, then, is a team? It is not a group. We advocate leaders asking their people this question from time to time, especially when dysfunctionality is occurring: are we a group or are we a team? Being clear on the difference is crucial.

Activity 6.1

If you are a leader, ask your team members this question. Note the answers, and be prepared to answer their almost inevitable response: what do you mean? Or, what's the difference? People, genuinely, have often never thought about this, so see Figure 6.1 to get a better sense of the distinction.

In brief, having a remit means we have a compelling reason for working together; interdependency implies that every member's contribution is needed and valued to achieve the objective; belief is self-explanatory, except to add that belief, negative or positive, has an extraordinary influence[5] on what happens in the physical world; and accountability is both to each other, that is within the team, and without, to the whole organisation.

Groups,[6] on the other hand, do none of the four components listed, or sometimes have them partially, or exercise them in a fragmented way. Indeed, ordinarily groups are no more than departmental titles: you work in sales, or admin, or marketing, or finance or any other department. Everyone there is working on similar work, but that does not make you part of a team. Perhaps the most significant aspect of being part of a group, and not belonging to a team, is this: the lack of accountability to the whole organisation, which means that groups tend to narrow their focus and never see the bigger picture of what the organisation is attempting to achieve; they 'silo' their efforts in other words, and often, bizarrely, by meeting the limited targets senior leadership has set, get rewarded for doing so!

But this is not for the real leader, or for anyone who wants to succeed at the highest level; besides which, when you are part of a team you always know it because there is an uptake of energy and excitement: you feel part of something, and not a cog in the wheel. A real team, then, is by its nature motivational.

Activity 6.2

As a preliminary exercise, consider any group/team that you lead, or are in, and ask yourself whether it is a group or team by checking whether there is:

(A)   A clear remit/mission   score out 10
(B)   Functional interdependency   score out 10
(C)   Belief in teamwork   score out 10
(D)   Accountability to each other and the organisation score out 10

Scores of 32 or above would indicate a high functioning team; below 32 to 24 would indicate some team qualities in place but some weaknesses; 23 to 14 would indicate typical group functioning; and below 14 shows group anarchy and little cohesion at all.

This, then, would provide an initial benchmark as to how we are doing … as a team. But as leaders we need more, and deeper, information. It is not enough in our experience either to think that things are just fine, and we are doing a great job. The capacity of the human mind, and the individual ego, to misinterpret reality[7] in their favour is vast, so we need independent ways of checking[8] how we are doing.

There are two really powerful and complementary ways we do this in Mapping Motivation, and they both build on what we have covered so far. First, and of primary importance, we need to do a Motivational Team Map to establish the profile of each individual.

Let's, therefore, consider the Motivational Team Map from the perspective of a leader. We have looked at Team Maps before in the Mapping Motivation series of books. But here is a new thing to consider: not all motivators are equal when considering building a team! This does not contradict our more general point that all motivators are equal, and that in any case context is everything. In this case the context is building the team. So the leader needs to be aware of what the potential pitfalls and advantages of a motivational type is in the team and individually.

Activity 6.3

If we think about the nine motivators, they are being either positive, neutral or difficult in terms of team building. In which categories would you allocate each of the nine motivators? For example, which of the nine motivators are likely to be pro-team building just because they are that motivator? Make a list. See Figure 6.2.

We need to clarify the rationale for these ideas. First, we think that the presence of Friend, Builder and Searcher motivator types[9] in any team will

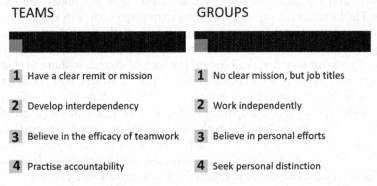

TEAMS	GROUPS
1 Have a clear remit or mission	1 No clear mission, but job titles
2 Develop interdependency	2 Work independently
3 Believe in the efficacy of teamwork	3 Believe in personal efforts
4 Practise accountability	4 Seek personal distinction

Figure 6.1 Four components of a real team

tend to strengthen and build the team – all things being equal.[10] What this means is that these motivators tend towards a team cohesion by virtue of the desires – the motivators – that they have. The Friend because they wish to belong, so perhaps the strongest motivator of all towards teamwork; the Searcher because of the realisation that making a difference can be more pronounced where there is team synergy; and, surprisingly and counter-intuitively, the Builder motivator. Actually, it is true to say that the Builder motivator can also be de-stabilising to team effectiveness, since the Builder motivator is the most individually competitive of all. But this must be set alongside the realisation that effective teams require a sense of achievement to function well. As Rosabeth Moss Canter[11] put it, "High performance may cause group cohesion and enjoyment as well as result from it; pride in the capacity and ability of others makes team work possible". Builders tend to be very goal and results orientated, and this can drive performance. So these three motivators tend to lead to people wanting to form a team.

On the other hand, the motivators which tend to work in the opposite direction are the Spirit, Director and Star. If we reflect on the nature of the desires of these three types it should be obvious why these types tend to want NOT to form teams (except, perhaps, under their own terms). Just as the Friend (R) is probably the strongest motivator tending towards teamwork, so the Spirit (G) is the strongest moving the individual away from being a team player. Before commenting on this further, it is important to stress that this does not mean they are 'bad' people, for that would be an unwarranted value judgement; but difficult, certainly and usually, and the fact is that they are necessary in many teams because they may bring to the 'party', that is to the team, something that is very important – context being everything again. For example, the Spirit, whilst definitely the most difficult to manage to lead type, may be the one member of a team who prevents it following into the folly of groupthink,[12] because their independence and autonomy may extend to their thinking also.

But to return: the Spirit, valuing freedom and autonomy, clearly can find teamwork and its associated commitments irksome, if not downright de-motivating. The Director per se, whilst wishing to manage high performance teams,[13] does not usually become a team player in them: their need to control and manage the team, even when they are not its leader, means that they can come across as pushy or superior. And finally, the Star, of course, wishing to shine and excel, can only do so at the expense of other team members, which often means that they incite resentment or envy from others. In short, the effective leader needs to account for this in any team profile, and be sure that the potential problems that we are identifying are mitigated, averted or, even better, resolved in a much more positive way. The question for the leader becomes: how do I deploy someone who wants freedom (Spirit), someone who wants my job (Director), someone who wants to outshine others (Star), effectively in this team?

The last group in this 'ease of team fit' is the 'neutral' category. Neutral is an important category because without neutrals there would only be polarisation; either for or against, as it were. But the neutral motivators supply, to use a musical analogy, the middle notes to complement and enhance the bass and the high ones. It is the neutral motivators that can really help us get to grips with all members of the team. Because they are more likely to 'float', or be perceived as 'floating' – think, 'floating voter' – then they appear more impartial, more objective, so more reasonable basically, and so more persuasive or influential to others. What we are talking about here is the way that influence works[14] between people.

Thus, we have the Creator, who can enjoy working with others on innovative projects and so be a team player, but also is equally equipped to be a loner who is the 'boffin'[15] who solves organisational problems – a sort of go-to individual who perpetually generates new ideas and solutions. The Expert, who too can be a 'boffin', but who on the one hand can be the type who enjoys teams and disseminating knowledge and ensuring learning, but on the other can be a know-it-all, aloof and superior to member of the team who does not know as much. And lastly, the Defender, who values processes and systems, and this can sometimes be at the expense of the individuals within the team – following rules takes precedence over common sense and valuing people.

So it should be clear that we are not saying that some motivators are simply anti-team; we are saying that there may be typical patterns of behaviour, driven by specific motivators, that may or may not support team building. In the case of the 'neutral', as we have seen, they can be great team players, but they also have a capacity to go equally in the other direction. The job of the leader is to get team cohesion, and to be fully aware of these issues.

Keeping in mind that we have analysed why there are three categories of motivators here that lead to ease of team fit, and also away from fit, let's look

	Positive team Motivators	Neutral team Motivators	Difficult team Motivators
R	Friend	Defender	Star
A	Builder	Expert	Director
G	Searcher	Creator	Spirit
	REWARDS		

Figure 6.2 Motivators and ease of team fit

at an overview (Figure 6.3) of all nine motivators in terms of their potential contribution to the cohesion of the team, and also potential pitfalls, even with the motivators most likely to want teamwork.

How does this apply in practice? Given the number of variables here, we have to be brief. So to go to the top, in Figure 6.4 we have a senior team Map of a FOOTSIE 250 company's three most senior figures: the CEO, the FD and the HR director; all leaders themselves but with special responsibility for the whole organisation and over 900 employees.

Activity 6.4

Study the Motivational Team Map in Figure 6.4. Note that these leaders are collectively 90% motivated, a high and good score. They are high energy people. But if we consider them as one team in themselves, and also as leaders of other teams within the organisation, what issues might be apparent from their Team Map? Make a list of what you think the salient points might be.

The most obvious thing, perhaps, to note is that the collective dominant motivator is Spirit! None of them has it as their personal number 1, but the underlying energy is for autonomy. Before considering anything else, then, the primary question would have to be: how well does this team work as a team? Of course, as consultants working with this team, that is exactly what was asked; and here we run into the first of many difficulties, for as George Binney[16] observed, "... part of the issue is the leader's willingness to scrutinise their own behaviour as hard as they do of other people". Getting leaders at a senior level to open up candidly, particularly in front of their peers, is or can be inordinately difficult.

	Potential major contribution to team	Potential pitfalls
SEARCHER	Meaning/Significance	Unrealistic idealism
BUILDER	Goals/Results	Internal competitiveness
FRIEND	Belonging/Unity	Co-dependency
CREATOR	Ideas/Fresh thinking	Innovation overload
EXPERT	Sound knowledge/Skills	Insularity
DEFENDER	Fairness/Stability	Change resistant
SPIRIT	Independent perspective/Boldness	Off-piste
DIRECTOR	Direction/Resourcing	Overstepping authority
STAR	Foregrounding issues/Personal touch	Resentment

Figure 6.3 Motivational contributions and issues for team work

Name		Spirit	Searcher	Expert	Creator	Defender	Builder	Director	Star	Friend	Motivation Audit			
											%	1	2	3
Max	MD	25	29	32	23	24	17	8	11	11	82%	8	8	9
Kitty	HR	31	21	8	10	22	31	31	16	10	88%	9	8	9
Daryl	FD	27	32	24	29	16	13	17	10	12	100%	10	10	10
Total		83	82	64	62	62	61	56	37	33	90%			

Figure 6.4 Senior team Map
Key: Dark grey – 1st motivator, middle grey – 2nd motivator, light grey – 3rd motivator, textured grey – lowest motivator

Second, we note that the MD and HR have two interesting, and opposite, Map profiles that will certainly make for interesting debates between them: Max (MD) is EX: top 32/40 and DI: low 8/40, whereas Kitty (HR) is DI: top 31/40 and EX: low 8/40. Almost an exact reversal; surprisingly, too, to find the MD so low in wanting to control, and so high in wanting to learn? And, equally, the HR director wanting to control, but not really interested in learning development. Not forgetting, they both share the need for autonomy, or not being bound by others! Either, then, this works really well on the adage of 'opposites attract', which is that complementarity or motivational diversity is a strength, or it is a total disaster in which seemingly *personalities* are constantly clashing, but which really is *motivational* energies conflicting.

Third, we also see that the FD is 100% motivated; always a result that gives even the optimist pause for thought. Too good to be true? Well, we can find out. Let's look at the whole Map for this individual and see if any anomaly is evident.

Activity 6.5

Look at Daryl's personal motivational numbers in Figure 6.5. Which, if any number(s), strike you as suspicious or cause for concern? Do you think this Map accurately portrays Daryl's true and full motivational profile?

Here is Daryl's personal Map – what we like to call his 22 numbers.[17] We see several things in this profile which are unusual, but strong: the top three motivators are well above average scoring (the average employee tends to have their top motivator scoring 24/40, whereas Daryl has three motivators above that); this suggests strong focus rather than balance. Also we see that the Growth motivators are overwhelmingly dominant; again, really unusual for an FD, since they tend to be more risk-averse. But the real statistics that jump out of us and say there is a false result here are the fact that all nine

Motivational Map Summary for Daryl, FD			
Motivator	Position	Score	PMA (/10)
Searcher	1	32	10
Creator	2	29	10
Spirit	3	27	10
Expert	4	24	10
Director	5	17	10
Defender	6	16	10
Builder	7	13	10
Friend	8	12	10
Star	9	10	10
PMA Score	100%		
Cluster Importance			
Relationship (R)	21%		
Achievement (A)	30%		
Growth (G)	49%		

Figure 6.5 Daryl's (FD) 22 numbers Map

motivators are scored 10/10 in terms of personal satisfaction. How likely is this to be true for anybody? That the motivators that are important to you as well as the ones that are unimportant are all being satisfied?

Rather, this seems an example of someone senior wanting not to appear demotivated in any way, and so all scoring is given the maximum possible in order, effectively, not to lose face with colleagues. So the motivators and their ordered sequence is probably correct and accurate, but we do not think that Daryl is 100% motivated; in other words, we think this Map does have false numbers in it and that appearing to be fully motivated is part of the false self-image Daryl wishes to perpetuate.

If we compare these numbers with Max, the MD, with even more face to lose, we see a very different set of results: these are likely to be true because they reflect how he is feeling about each motivator; overall, the scoring is high, but there is a recognition in the results that some motivators are not as high as they might be. For example, in Max's top four (Figure 6.6) Defender – security – is only 7/10. Actually, given how precarious life can be at Board level at the top, that does seem very realistic. But note as a matter of fundamental importance: the MD has Director as his lowest motivator (8/40, so an 'inverse spike' or what is the beginning

Motivational Map Summary for Max, MD			
Motivator	Position	Score	PMA (/10)
Expert	1	32	8
Searcher	2	29	8
Spirit	3	25	9
Defender	4	24	7
Creator	5	23	7
Builder	6	17	7
Star	7	11	7
Friend	8	11	8
Director	9	8	8
PMA Score	82%		
Cluster Importance			
Relationship (R)	26%		
Achievement (A)	31%		
Growth (G)	43%		

Figure 6.6 Max, MD, 22 Numbers

of an aversion to that motivator), so he is certainly not driven to manage, although he may have the skill set to do so. Over the long term, however, we tend to do what we want to do, rather than what we need to do. This, then, is an important point to take up either with the team or the individual or both.

Thus, to return to the big picture, the senior management team of three (Figure 6.4), the effective working of this team as a team is the issue that the Maps outline. We see three individuals, highly motivated, likely to be highly effective, but with some opposing motivators and with the Spirit common to them all. Despite denying it, as is likely in the case of the FD, they are almost certainly a group who could achieve more as a team. Given the need of at least the FD to conceal his true motivators, the starting point for re-building this particular team would be through a coaching programme that was personal,[18] and then which led into some collective team training.

We come, then, to an important further development of The Five Elements Model that we outlined earlier in Chapters 4 and 5. For whilst the team Motivational Map is extraordinarily accurate, because it deals with energy, it can sometimes seem abstruse and remote from the everyday practicalities of work; we stress: it's absolutely not remote, but can seem so to busy executives unfamiliar with the concepts underpinning it. Therefore, we like to introduce another diagnostic tool that we have developed and which has even more of an initial impact. This is The Five Elements Team Performance Questionnaire (see Figure 6.7).

Given, as we have explained, that any outcome that we want goes through The Five Elements of Visioning (V), Planning (P), Facilitating (F), Doing (D) and Checking (C), then a team will also need, consciously or otherwise, to follow that sequence through in its activities. Remember, too, that in Chapter 4, Figure 4.8, we suggested that each individual had a preference, and second backup, style their deployment of V, P, F, D, and C. This means that we can establish how effective a team is by getting feedback on how each component of this systematic process is being undertaken. But, with one caveat!

We have noticed again and again that simply having a process, good and complete as it might be, is not enough: the fact is, people can understand a process, want to deliver a process, but find themselves incapable of doing so! In other words, the crux of the matter is that The Five Elements have to be driven, and the only thing that will drive them is effective leadership. So our questionnaire, then, includes 14 questions that incorporate all 5 Elements, plus adds one simple question to establish how well led the team is. Without the team members buying into their own leader's competence and ability, not much is going to be achieved however good the 'system' is.

Activity 6.6

It is critically important to find out how well your team is performing. The questionnaire below (Figure 6.7) covers the six key areas that lead to effective team functioning: 1) Leadership (L) + The Five Elements (VPFDC) 2) Vision, 3) Planning, 4) Facilitating (Resourcing), 5) Doing (taking Action), 6) Checking (Evaluating). Consider your current team, whether you lead it or not, or any team that you have belonged to in the past, and score each question. Don't agonise over the scoring, but put the number that seems to come to you.

This questionnaire is very tough[19] – especially if you lead the team! The first question is searching. Furthermore, research indicates that leaders tend to over-rate themselves.[20] What do your team members think? The interpretation of your individual score is:

120–150 – team is very good and highly effective (80+%)

90–119 – team has good qualities and needs tweaking to optimise performance (60+%)

52–89 – serious structural weaknesses and areas needing a whole review (35+%)

0–51 – team is not a team at all, but a 'group' – a fundamental distinction (<35%)

		Score / 10 comment	
	For each question score out of 10 is maximum. 10 means excellently or the best possible; 1 or even 0 means very bad or the worst! As an aide-memoire, you may wish to add a brief comment alongside the score in order to ttiflesh outttj some detail on the meaning of your score.		
1	How effectively is the team led?		L
2	How decisive are we?		V
3	How good are we at initiating action?		V
4	How clear are our objectives?		V
5	How good are we at analysing problems?		P
6	Do we concentrate sufficiently on priorities?		P
7	How well do we plan in detail?		P
8	How well do we work together?		F
9	Does everyone contribute?		F
10	To what extent can people speak their minds?		F
11	If conflict - is it openly expressed and about issues?		F&D
12	Are we well supported in our work?		D
13	Are our efforts consistently co-ordinated?		D
14	Do we regularly review our progress?		C
15	Do we check that we did what we said we'd do?		C

Figure 6.7 The Five Elements team performance questionnaire

The above gives you an instant 'fix' on where you (individually) perceive your team to be, that is, performance-wise as a team. Clearly, this is just 'your' perception, but it becomes a lot more than that when other team members' perceptions are added to the mix; then, we start to get a real view of what is going on in the team at an accomplishment level (already having established the motivational drives).

Before we analyse this, note: we have included a blank column, R4, just to indicate and remind readers that this team can include any number of Respondents (R); the average score for each question, given in the last column, is divided by the number of Respondents (in this case, 3) and the figure is rounded either up or down to a whole number. Also, note that one question, number 11, is classified as a crossover question: it has its feet, as it were, in two camps: dealing with conflict is clearly a facilitation issue, if ever there were one, but equally it is about actually doing something, which in this case is in ensuring that conflict does not remain covert, unexpressed and irrelevant to the needs of the organisation. Finally, because the total scores are out of 150, we think it is easier to read the significance of the numbers as a percentage, and the collective totals out of 10.

Activity 6.7

Study Figure 6.8 and its numbers: what are the five most important points that you can see or deduce from these scorings?

First, that the team is not optimal as a team: that would require an overall score of over 80%. But at 73% they have many good qualities in place. So the question becomes: how does the leader improve this team functioning?

Second, in terms of leadership (question 1) they rate themselves 8/10, above their own average for the whole cycle (7/10). Interestingly, the actual Leader, Max, rates himself more highly than the others rate him. Kitty has a more

DATE						
Question	Max MD	Kitty HR	Daryl FD	R4	Total	Average - :- R = 3
1 L	9	6	8		23	8
2 V	9	6	10		25	8
3 V	7	6	10		23	8
4 V	10	8	10		28	9
5 P	10	7	10		27	9
6 P	6	4	8		18	6
7 P	8	7	8		23	8
8 F	5	3	6		14	5
9 F	7	5	10		22	7
10 F	10	6	10		26	7
11 F&D	8	6	10		24	8
12 D	8	9	6		23	8
13 D	6	6	4		16	5
14 C	6	6	6		18	6
15 C	6	6	6		18	6
Total	115	91	122		328	108
x2-:- 3=%	77%	61%	81%		73%	7

Figure 6.8 The five elements team performance analysis sheet

sanguine view: is that because she knows better, or is it because her number one motivator is Director and she feels she could do a better job?

Third, the FD is again perhaps showing his 'top side' rather than what he actually believes. The bold 10/10s, for example on question 2 may indicate that he sees himself as 'decisive', which is not perhaps the same as 'we' being decisive. So this needs more investigation.

Fourth, consider the lowest scores as vital Achilles' Heels that need repair: question 8, a Facilitation question, scored 5 (How well do we work together?); question 13, a Doing question, also scored 5, (Are our efforts consistently coordinated?); and then there are three questions scoring 6 each: questions, 6 (Do we concentrate sufficiently on priorities?), a Planning question, and questions 14 and 15, (Do we regularly review our progress? and Do we check that we did what we said we'd do?), both Checking questions.

Fifth, therefore (following on from the fourth point), there is a pattern emerging: The L, V, and P aspects of their work are generally ranked highly; but it is once we get into F, then D and C, that aspects of the work are less satisfactory. Question 5 and 11 are highly correlated, since they involve working together and coordination; and perhaps the priority failure in question 6 may be about the priority of team working, which is never fully addressed.

Thus, the leader – Max in this case – here is beginning to see some primary work that needs to be done if this team is to sustain its energy, collaborate more effectively, and accomplish all that needs to be done.

We will end this chapter with two simple tools that can help the leadership sort out its own functionality[21] as a team.

Activity 6.8

Bring together the team you currently lead or are in. Simultaneously work together on these questions. This is using what is called the Role Negotiation Technique.[22]

1 List what expectations you have of others in the team
2 Focus on what you feel others should do more or better, do less or stop doing, or maintain
3 Exchange lists and negotiate with each other

Agree on which behaviours should be changed and which need to be maintained. Circulate a master list of agreements to the team later. To help make this clearer, see and use Figure 6.9.

This exercise, of course, requires openness, honest and high degrees of trust; it also requires that we leave the ego slumbering in bed, and not up and about like a roaring lion. If the leader of a team seriously thinks that this is not a

TEAM	DO BETTER	DO MORE OF	DO LESS OF	STOP DOING	MAINTAIN AS IS
MAX					
KITTY					
DARYL					

Figure 6.9 Role expectations of team members

do-able exercise,[23] then there is no team at all, and only a group from which one must begin a complete reconstruction.

Fortunately, having done these two diagnostics in this chapter – the Senior Team Map (Figure 6.4) and The Five Elements Team Performance Questionnaire (Figure 6.7) it should be apparent that the scores of both or either give some indication as to the suitability of using the Role Negotiation Technique. In the case of the senior team of Max, Kitty and Daryl we have scores of 90% (team Map) and 73% (The Five Elements) and so there is plenty of good energy, effective functionality, to enable the role technique to work. But what if the scores for Team Maps and five Elements Team Performance are both below 60%? Or worse, both below 35%?

To be clear, there is no one easy solution, one infallible technique – not least because any technique or idea has to be applied by someone (or some ones, plural!) who may not fully understand it or apply it effectively.[24] It is worth noting that all management techniques when applied mechanically tend to have a deadening effect on staff.

But we have a process called Motivational Facilitation which we have used time and time again to get results from highly dysfunctional teams. This process predicates the central importance of motivation, as you might expect, but uses motivation without specific reference to the Motivational Maps, although as an extra feature, the Maps can be brought in to add even more depth to the experience.

How does Motivational Facilitation work? The first thing is to build up a sense of the importance of team work, collaboration, and the power of synergies. What is the starting point for this? The client or customer, of course! We need to ask our team/group what is the next big project or task we have to do for our client?

Our next big client project is ....

Identifying a specific project or work assignment is important because it gets us beyond generalities and theories: this is what is on the table, and this is what is at stake.

Second, we need to get them independently to consider what the outcomes for the client/customer would be if we all worked together as a team.

If we could work together as a team the results for our client on this big project would be..

Considering what would happen if we all were a team is a wonderfully 'dreamy' kind of exercise; most team members like it. It generates enthusiasm even if at some deep subconscious level each person is saying, 'Yea, but we'll never be one with him/her in charge'. What would happen if we *were* a team usually looks marvellous because we all see that it will lead to outstanding performance levels.

But following this, we need to ask the opposite.

If we do not work together as a team the results for our client on this big project will be..

These last reflections, on not being a team, tend to be a complete downer, but also a rather vivid wake-up call. Actually, it's horrific – what might be the results for our client? Panic! And if there is an actual historic example of just this, now would be the time to remind everyone of it and its consequences. At this point, then, we are now ready to undertake the Motivational Facilitation because everyone in the team/group is fully aware of the importance of being a real team, not because of wanting team work, but because of the consequences of the alternative.

Activity 6.9

Stage 1

With a flipchart or whiteboard to hand, ask everyone to write down what, when working on this next project, would be the top five motivators for them. To be clear, we are not asking for them to identify their Motivational Map profiles; we are asking what their top five motivators are in the most specific sense of 'motivator' to them. So, for example, the most motivating thing about work is when we go for a pizza on Friday lunchtimes; or, when I hit target and get commission on my sales; or, when a customer writes a letter to my boss praising my service to her. And so on.

(The extra Map feature here that we referred to earlier, and which is optional, is that if your team know about Motivational Maps, then get them to try to identify which of the nine motivators underpins each of their five top motivators. 'We' going for the pizza on Fridays, for example, may well be the Friend motivator.)

Stage 2

Now do the same for the five top de-motivators. Get everyone to list their five top de-motivators when they work on a project. This, too, needs to be specific. Though sometimes one word says it all: criticism (as in, I don't like it, for example).

Stage 3

The facilitator of this session, which could be the leader or an external facilitator, now treats the top five motivators and five de-motivators. Asking each team member in turn, the leader writes down on the flip chart/whiteboard their answers. If we were dealing with Max, Kitty and Daryl, there would then be 15 motivators on 1 board (and then subsequently 15 de-motivators). Now comes the challenge, the facilitator invites the team members to reduce the total number of motivators (or subsequently de-motivators) to only 5, and here's the catch: only the person who stated the motivator (de-motivator) can authorise its removal from the list. With only 15 on the board this may seem do-able, but if we had a team of 10, then there would be 50 posts to reduce to 5!

The keys to enabling this to happen are:

a   ensuring when posting the motivators/de-motivators to link like or similar ideas together. People have different ways of expressing their preferences and aversions, which on reflection they can agree mean more or less the same thing. So that sometimes two, or three, or even four or five posts may reduce to one example. For example, sharing a pizza on a Friday, spending social time with colleagues, liking each other's company, and so on might all be agreed as constituting one idea;

b   realising that in giving people power they often give it back to you; and they do this when you say to them, Look, John, Jo has rated 'recognition' as being important to her, but you have 'training'. How do you rate that – how does recognition compare for you? Strange thing about doing this, is that many times people had not considered some other option or alternative, and knowing that it is important to somebody else, they frequently give way, and say something like: 'Actually, I hadn't thought about recognition. That's important to me too, so I'd prefer you to include it in the final five'.

Once you have the top five motivators and top five de-motivators, all agreed by and through the group/team, you are in an ideal position to create the team agreement. Keep in mind, this is an agreement only for the next 'big project'. It is context specific. Everybody is bound by it; it should be displayed prominently for all to see continually.

A team agreement might look something like this.

We agree to	We agree to avoid
Value the input of each team member irrespective of their position or role	Blaming others and scapegoating
Support and nurture all contributions that help us solve problems	Inconsistency in words and actions
Develop listening skills and demonstrate open-mindedness and mutual respect	Manipulation of others
Support team decisions and honour confidentiality	Creating 'inner teams' ' or in-groups' within the team
Seek to deliver on all our promises and commitments	Withholding important information from other members
Signed and dated by all the members	

Figure 6.10 Draft Team Agreement

This is a very powerful document, and three more points need to be made about it. First, if you were to look at all the motivators/de-motivators that are listed on the boards, you would almost certainly find a mixture of task and people types.[25] But invariably, when it gets down to what's really important or not to people, it is invariably about people and how they are treated.

Second, in a truly dysfunctional team there may be someone who doesn't want to sign. In our experience this is rare, but it is possible, and that should be respected. But the minimum mutual respect that should be extended to one who does not wish to sign the agreement is that they provide a reason why. That reason why is all you will need to know in order to know what to do in future.

Third, to take the whole process a stage further, consider this: what three major commitments to action will I undertake when I resume work? Given they have all agreed to work in a new way via the Team Agreement, now is the opportunity to get even more buy-in with specific commitments. And as we consider those individual commitments to action, we come to Chapter 8 where the issue of leadership and the individual is of paramount importance.

This is a very long chapter already, but we think necessarily so, given the importance of leadership in building teams. We have tried to show and shared what we consider to be extremely powerful tools, techniques and ideas that enable the leader to get that cohesion, that commitment, that unity that so defines great teams; and it should be obvious that this is not easy, because people are not easy. But going about this activity in the right way can produce outstanding results.

But we have to say – so there is a rider – that there are some people who can never be leaders whether they technically have that role (so have 'position power' – see Chapter 5) now or are aspiring to be leaders in future as part of their career advancement. Because we are experts in motivation we frequently get the response from all levels within an organisation, but especially from the top, that we must be 'flaky', or 'hippy', or 'soft' or ineffective somehow because all this is 'soft' stuff, and the real work is concentrated on the cash flow and the sales; and the idea that we are 'soft' creates the impression that we want everyone to be in a 'hippy' place where we all love each other – are motivated – and no hard decisions about people are ever made. Nothing could be further from the truth as the next chapter, Chapter 7, is going to show.

How do Motivational Maps help us address issues with the leader who simply cannot lead? Read on!

Notes

1 Kenneth W Thomas in the USA writes: "What this means is that measuring the value-added of leadership boils down to measuring improvements in a team's achievements of task purposes, it's work quality, and its motivation", *Intrinsic Motivation at Work*, Barrett-Koehler (2009). Also, from the USA, Patrick Lencioni writes, "Not finance. Not strategy. Not technology. It is teamwork that remains the ultimate competitive advantage, both because it is so powerful and so rare". *The Five Dysfunctions of a Team*, Jossey-Bass (2002). And in the UK, William Kendall who built the massively successful Green and Blacks chocolate company says, "Building a vibrant company is about forming a good team... You cannot do it on your own ... It is a question of persuading people who are better than you to form a successful team", cited in *MoneyWeek*, 24 June 2016.
2 *Mapping Motivation*, James Sale, Routledge (2016), Chapter 6.
3 This is not to denigrate Christ in any way; one is considering this case purely as an example of management, not in the spiritual sense. The leadership of Jesus Christ (and believers would say the subsequent promptings of the Holy Spirit) enabled the team to be created and developed in the first place. But note how with virtually all major religions there seems to be some charismatic founder who then hands on the torch to a 'team' of disciples, and these achieve the full flowering of the movement that does not happen whilst the founder is actually alive. Teams are wonderful, then!
4 To use an Eastern religious source: Lao Tzu writing in the *Tao Te Ching*, "When the best leader's work is done the people say, 'We did it ourselves'". And also, "If a wholly Great One rules the people hardly know that he exists". *Tao Te Ching*, from the Richard Wilhelm edition, translated into English by H G Ostwald, Arkana, Penguin (1985). And this ties in with: "A leader, then, is a person who is orientated towards results more than power or social relations ... the results-orientated leader does not dictate the methods for achieving the results and, moreover, does not need to claim the victories as their own" – Jan Carlzon, *Moments of Truth*, Harper Business (1987, 2001).
5 "Belief creates the actual fact" – William James, *The Will to Believe and Other Essays in Popular Philosophy* (1897), "Is Life Worth Living?" Republished, CreateSpace Independent Publishing Platform (2017).

6 For more details on the meaning of these four components, see *Mapping Motivation*, ibid.

7 As the ancient Greek Demosthenes observed, "The easiest thing of all is to deceive one's self; for what a man wishes he generally believes to be true". Cited by Cynthia Bove, *The Fifth Disciple: Choose Again and Find True Happiness*, John Hunt Publishing; Reprint edition (2011).

8 So, we are with The Five Elements model C1 question: where are we now?

9 Notice the symmetry unfolding here: that the three positive, three neutral and three difficult team-forming motivators contain one each from the Relationship, Achievement and Growth categories.

10 This 'all things being equal' – is an important qualification. We have referred before, for example, to low self-esteem and game playing individuals whose map profiles may be accurate but irrelevant to how they behave. See, *Mapping Motivation for Coaching*, James Sale and Bevis Moynan, Routledge (2018). Other factors too can complicate the situation, not least of all the fact that people are not driven by one motivator solely; there is a complex interplay of motivators, and so someone, for example, with Friend as their number one motivator, may have 2 other motivators at second and third place which tend to obviate the Friend drive, especially if closely scored together. Say, Friend (first), Spirit (second) and Director (third) – this would be a mixed combination of motivators that would take some careful scrutiny to unpick.

11 Rosabeth Moss Kanter, *When Giants Learn to Dance*, Free Press: New edition (1990)

12 We touched on groupthink in Mapping Motivation, ibid. Five danger signs of Groupthink are: 1) Incomplete surveys of alternative, so re-enforcement of current ways of working; 2) Incomplete survey of goals, so line of least resistance taken; 3) Failure to examine risks, either a. inherent in current ways of doing things, or b. in proposals for change; 4) Poor information search, so team restricts its search for information; 5) Selective bias in processing information, leading to looking for a quick-fix and its confirmation. These are all dangers leaders should seek to avoid; the motivational composition of their team can be extremely useful here.

13 This, of course, is the ultimate paradox: those most wanting to manage are most likely to not form strong teams! Special note and care must be taken of this point.

14 Robert Cialdini, *Influence: The Psychology of Persuasion*, Harper Business (Revised, 2007). Cialdini identifies six core sources of influence/compliance: social proof, authority, consistency, reciprocity, liking and scarcity. In the context in which we are speaking, having 'neutrals' in the team can help provide the especially necessary 'social proof', which is to say when in Rome do as the Romans do, and authority. Clearly, consistency, reciprocity and liking may also play their parts.

15 According to Wikipedia: "Boffin is a British slang term for a scientist, engineer, or other person engaged in technical or scientific research and development. A 'boffin' was generally viewed by the regular services as odd, quirky or peculiar, though quite bright and essential to helping in the war effort. The World War II conception of boffins as war-winning researchers lends the term a more positive connotation than related terms such as nerd, egghead, geek or spod" https://bit.ly/2E8v9x8. Although scientist-types were the target for original application of the word, it has come more generally to refer to any sort of creative or geeky solution finder.

16 George Binney and Colin Williams, *Leaning into the Future*, Nicolas Brealey (1995).

17 See *Mapping Motivation for Coaching*, ibid, for a lot more on this.

18 For more on using the Maps in a coaching context and some great questions to use based on Map profiles and the 22 numbers, see *Mapping Motivation for Coaching*, ibid.

19 We should add that when we distribute this questionnaire to team members we remove all reference to The Five Elements and of L, the leadership, for the simple reason of their not trying to second guess what they are answering.

20 For example, research on 11,000 people revealed that 33% leaders overestimated their leadership ability, about 45% leaders were not trusted as much as they thought. The Professional Manager 9.3. More recently, a study by Hay Group's McClelland Center finds that senior leaders in an organization often gain power at the expense of self-knowledge, and are more likely to overrate themselves in self-awareness, self-management and social skills. Michelle M Smith, https://bit.ly/2FAt8rV (2018).

21 Keep in mind here that we are not attempting, because we have not got the space, to cover all the issues that the actual analyses of the Motivational Maps and The Five Elements threw up: so, for example, the Checking question and how we introduce more effective evaluation into our processes is obviously vital.

22 "Another technique for effective team building developed by Roger Harrison is called the Role Negotiation Technique. Sometimes people in a team are unwilling to change because it would mean a loss of power or influence to the individual. This resistance to change causes team ineffectiveness. Role negotiation techniques are often used to great advantage in such situations" – Kushboo Sinha, *Techniques Used in Building Team Performance*, https://bit.ly/2PxDBbb.

23 There may be several reasons why it is not 'do-able', but certainly a common one is the perception that fellow team members are not emotionally resilient, or intellectually honest, enough, to address the real issues at this stage in their development. Add to that the fact that some leaders wish to avoid what they see as unnecessary conflict.

24 And equally, let's be aware of the serial game players who no matter what is done sabotage the endeavour or project. Once identified, the only question for these is how can be best remove them from our organisation. For more on this see Chapter 6 of *Mapping Motivation for Coaching*, ibid.

25 For more on task and people, see John Adair, *Effective Leadership*, Pan; Main Market edition (2009). Essentially, Adair proposed that a leader needs to: get the task done; ensure the group doing it works effectively – sustaining morale and motivation; and cater for individual needs – attempting to dovetail these with the needs of the task and of the group. When all three areas overlapped, then the leader was doing their job properly. Our own model could be seen as an expansion of this: getting the job done is thinking and doing, ensuring the group works is our team building, and catering for individual needs is our motivating the individual. Underpinning everything, of course, and which Adair amply recognises, is that '+1', that commitment to one's own personal development.

Chapter 7

When leadership isn't

A 360° Maps case study

We have come a long way in considering leadership, and covered a lot of ground. It is important to repeat what we said at the outset: we are not providing a comprehensive coverage of all that is involved in the leadership function, for that would require several weighty tomes, if it could be achieved at all. No, rather we are considering leadership from – in our opinion – the highly underappreciated and little understood perspective of motivation and motivation's integral and essential connection with leadership. And in all these deliberations we are showing how the Motivational Maps and its cognate tools provide unique insight and solutions for leaders faced with pressing motivational problems within their respective organisations.

It is timely therefore in this penultimate chapter to consider a case study in which we return to the issue of Motivational 360° Team Maps, which we first explored in *Mapping Motivation for Engagement*[1] and followed up with Susannah Brade-Waring's study in Chapter 3 of this book. Now, sadly, however, we want to look at how using this Mapping Motivation technology can help us identify and remove leaders who really should never be leaders.

The problem is, as every organisation knows: we appoint people to senior positions because they talk the talk, seem to know what they are doing, have impressive CVs, great references, and they dazzle us at interview. Being great at interviews, however, is frequently not the same as being great at the job. In Chapter 5 of our book, *Mapping Motivation for Engagement* we provide a methodology for recruitment using Motivational Maps that seriously helps put the odds in favour of selecting the right candidate. But even at its best we are talking about moving the chances from 50–50 to 70–30 or 80–20.[2] In short, we can always make a mistake. But let us not make the fundamental error of thinking that because we are and wish to be motivational, that this means we cannot hold people to account for their performance, or that we have to be 'nice' to people and not upset them, because that would be de-motivational, or that we cannot probe into the heart of the matter.

Indeed, this 'probing into the heart of the matter' is exactly what Motivational Maps are designed to do, for we remember Maps, quintessentially, are about making the 'invisible, visible'. It is to try to see what is really going on in the human being who is 'leading' (or not) for us. And it is important, therefore, that Maps help inform us when clearly things are not going well and we want to know why. We have, then, a case study in which the Maps were decisive in enabling an organisation to remove a leader; and this too is motivational, because it frees both the organisation and the leader to be removed to advance in their growth and in their careers, whereas the wrong leader in the wrong organisation merely leads to blockage and stalemate.

Alpha HD Security Plus (AHDSP) are specialists in monitoring systems, using HD cameras to observe workflow, customer behaviour and security over the internet; they have traded for over 20 years and are based in south Birmingham. They recruited Alan into the role of Operations Manager; a pivotal leadership role whose purpose is to ensure that the Sales, Service, Installation and Admin teams all work effectively together, which was not happening. To add to this, invoices were not being released on time or chased up, causing a cash flow problem at the end of each month. The accounting system didn't seem to be picking up the invoicing problems; Alan needed to look at options available to the business to make sure that accurate invoicing and collection happened. Alan was also given the challenging tasks of looking at staff accountability, reviewing company policies and updating its procedures. Plus, whilst achieving these objectives he was also tasked with looking at revenue generation for AHDSP. Quite a tall order then!

A number of points need to be made about this context. First, Alan came across extremely well at interview and had a seemingly good and comparable track record in this field. Jane Thomas, co-author, is an advisory consultant to this company, but was not involved in this particular appointment. Second, the appointment required two quite different skillsets: on the one hand, the ability to form and motivate strong teams (see Chapters 6 and 8) and on the other to do the 'hard' stuff – get accounting systems working, review policies and so on. And third, that Alan didn't see his key objectives as overly challenging, having had experience in delivering these for previous clients; and he thought that forming good working relationships with the staff was one of his strengths. He relished the idea of bringing the teams together for the benefit of the organisation and its overall productivity. At the moment of his appointment, then, both the CEO and Alan were happy about the prospect of what Alan might do for this business, and Alan seemed to be brimming with confidence and ability.

Jane Thomas at that point suggested that in starting at AHDSP Alan did a Motivational Map, Figure 7.1.

Activity 7.1

Imagine that you are the CEO of AHDSP and having appointed Alan, you are now reviewing his Motivational Map in Figure 7.1. What three significant issues or pointers emerge from studying his 22 numbers?

Motivational Map Summary for Alan First Motivational Map after being recruited			
Motivator	**Position**	**Score**	**PMA (/10)**
Searcher	1	29	9
Friend	2	25	9
Defender	3	23	9
Creator	4	23	10
Spirit	5	19	9
Director	6	17	8
Expert	7	17	7
Star	8	14	10
Builder	9	13	8
PMA Score	90%		
Cluster Importance			
Relationship (R)	35%		
Achievement (A)	26%		
Growth (G)	39%		

Figure 7.1 Alan's first Motivational Map

Jane Thomas was tasked by the CEO with initially meeting Alan to give him feedback on his Map profile, shortly after he had been recruited. He had been a Business Consultant, but was now looking at a more stable and secure job; also, he wanted to be part of a team having previously been mainly working on his own. Clearly, her job was to build Alan up and strengthen and empower him by focusing on motivational strengths:

1   That he was 90% motivated, which implied high levels of energy
2   That he wanted to make a difference for the company more than anything else, so Jane could discuss the HOW of realising that drive
3   That Friend – the drive to belong – was his second most powerful motivator, and so this potentially boded well for his need to be part of a team, and by being/becoming a 'friend' to those he managed,[3] he would be able to create a stronger sense of cohesion and purpose.

All this was good. But as a mapper, Jane also noticed three other things that were not necessary to share with Alan at this stage, if at all in future:

4   He was charged with ensuring that invoices were paid in a timely fashion and also of improving revenue generation, but his lowest motivator was the Builder, which obviously means that money matters were his least important consideration from his motivational point of view

5   His top four motivators were conflicting in terms of direction: the Searcher and Creator were highly change and risk friendly, whereas his Friend and Defender motivators were highly change and risk averse. The scoring for there were (29+23) =52 and (25+23) =48 respectively, so very close

6   In the actual Cluster analysis (the RAG) the Achievement motivators (Expert, Builder, Director) were significantly the lowest at 26%. Could Alan be a 'friendly idealist' who lacked the punch to actually get things done from a business perspective?

With Jane's feedback on his Motivational Map, as well as Jane showing him the Map profiles of his team members and senior staff, Alan could, first, increase his own self-awareness and second reflect on the way he might work with the staff and senior leadership. From this he set up an individual meeting with the senior team to understand their view of the business requirements; and found these did vary. The senior leadership seemed, individually, to be pulling in different directions. This was not benefiting the organisation nor the interpersonal relationships with staff; and this was confirmed when he met with the staff, who said the same. To be clear: the senior staff were good and committed people, but they were sending mixed messages to Alan, a fact which had to be taken into account in considering Alan's performance.

Supplementing his understanding of the Motivational Maps, Jane then introduced Alan to a number of leadership models to help him get to grips with his staff and his tasks. The first of these, emerging from Jane's clear concerns from what points 5 and 6 above, is the High Challenge, High Support Mind-set.[4] This model can help leaders see where they are on the important spectrums of achievement (being challenged) and support. How did he see himself as a leader? And how did he view himself on that spectrum as being led? Finally, clearly, being highly challenging and highly supportive, as well as experiencing that, were the optimum conditions for serious success; so how could one challenge more, yet be more supportive too?

Perhaps, unsurprisingly, Jane found the results of this model in Figure 7.2 slightly concerning, and more aligned to her unexpressed concerns in points 4–6 above. Alan saw himself as highly challenging and highly supportive as a leader; in other words, he was in an optimum place. But he saw his own leaders as being not challenging enough: if we recall his objectives were not 'overly challenging'. And he also saw them as not being overly supportive either: they were pulling in different directions, so there were more mixed messages coming through.

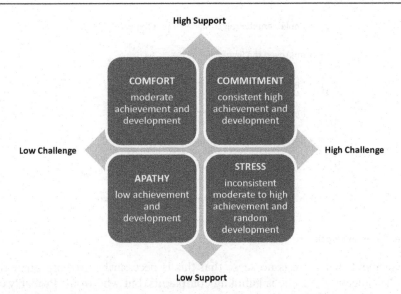

Figure 7.2 Leadership support and challenge

Jane immediately saw the danger here, the danger she had encountered so many times before, and which all organisations have experienced: 'I am alright Jack; it's everybody else who is the problem'! The ego moves centre stage, and this means everybody else *is* the problem. But the essence of being a true leader, as we have laboured to say, is taking account of oneself[5] and doing something about it. This is the most difficult situation for any organisation to address because it requires fundamental and personal change: a whole change in attitude for one thing, and an openness to a new way – a people-centric way – of doing things. As well, we need to say at this point, it requires high levels of self-esteem to be able to accept this; and this issue comes back to the '+1' element of leadership that we developed in Chapters 2 and 3, and which we said were the most essential aspect of all.

Various actions were taken during the course of Alan's first six months at AHDSP, and at the end of it a number of things became clearer. Some staff had lost respect for Alan, and the CEO himself found meeting with Alan extremely draining. A list of positives, negatives and a developmental action points was compiled.

Activity 7.2

Reviewing his positive achievements in Figure 7.3, what do you notice about them that is especially important?

The most notable thing about Alan's achievements in Figure 7.3 is that the achievements are all task orientated. True, he has set up regular reviews for

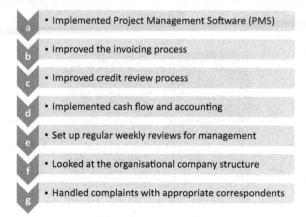

Figure 7.3 Alan's positives

management, but there is no sense that this is necessarily anything other than 'another' meeting. Yes, he is handling complaints, but who from? Probably customers, not staff. What is absent here is the sense of his impacting the employees, his staff; and there is a good reason for this as we see in the negatives.

Activity 7.3

Reviewing his areas for concern (negatives) in Figure 7.4, what is the clear issue here? And given this situation, what would you recommend as a solution or way of moving forward for it?

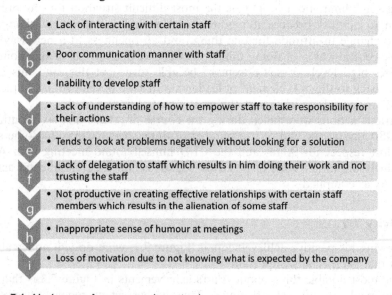

Figure 7.4 Alan's areas for concern (negatives)

Just as the positives were more or less all task or 'thing'-orientated, so here we have the reverse: all the problems stem from his handling or mishandling of the employees, and ultimately this ongoing scenario has led to point i. in Figure 7.4: loss of motivation. The energy and enthusiasm is draining out of Alan as he wrestles unsuccessfully with the people in his organisation. He came in quite blasé about what needed to be done, obviously underestimated the scale of the challenge, and now would appear to be in deep trouble. For the positives of Figure 7.3, if one is being honest, are nowhere near as important as the negatives: the things done do not offset the employees being under-deployed, demotivated, disengaged and fractious. He has addressed short-term and immediate issues, but long-term trouble is building up. In answer to the question, then, what solution might there be to this, one answer would be simply: dismiss him! But this option must be weighed against the overall situation, the potential for change, and the fact that he has in the 'hard' areas of the business got some very good results. This person, then, should be invested in and developed further; at least, that was the decision of the CEO, although Jane did express some reservations from seeing Alan's first Map. But clearly, for the CEO to dismiss Alan now would be an admission that he had made a wrong appointment – made a mistake, in fact, and most people, never mind CEOs, wish to avoid such an admission!

The actual areas for development were identified as follows in Figure 7.5 and every single point is about developing staff, including where we want to get Alan to get staff to use the software that he has set up. However, the underlying aim is to develop Alan himself to make him capable of delivering on this.

It was decided to re-map Alan as the CEO was getting increasingly concerned about Alan's motivation. Jane also explained that it would be useful

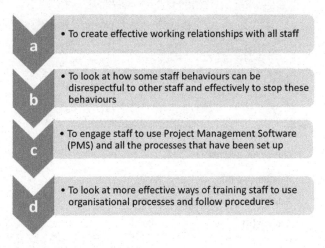

a
- To create effective working relationships with all staff

b
- To look at how some staff behaviours can be disrespectful to other staff and effectively to stop these behaviours

c
- To engage staff to use Project Management Software (PMS) and all the processes that have been set up

d
- To look at more effective ways of training staff to use organisational processes and follow procedures

Figure 7.5 Alan's areas for development

for development and feedback for Alan to look at a 360° feedback from the Directors and some of the staff. This to Jane seemed the most powerful way to affect Alan's behaviours: to have a direct insight into how staff viewed him.

Activity 7.4

Compare Alan's second map in Figure 7.6 with his first in Figure 7.1. Identify three significant changes in his motivational profile.

This profile was startling in comparison with his initial Map: first, his PMA had gone from 90% to 49%. He was becoming de-motivated and had entered the motivational Risk Zone;[6] this was already accurately being picked up by the CEO. Jane was interested to see from the Motivational 360° Team feedback if any staff were also aware of this.

Second, there has been a complete reversal of his basic motivational stance: his lowest Builder, which was reasonably satisfied (8/10) is now his top motivator but seriously unsatisfied (3/10); his second top motivator, Friend, which highly satisfied (9/10) is now second lowest and deeply unsatisfied (4/10); and just to round off with one more extreme example, his Star, his second lowest

Motivational Map Summary for Alan Second Motivational Map			
Motivator	Position	Score	PMA (/10)
Builder	1	24	3
Searcher	2	23	8
Creator	3	22	7
Defender	4	19	6
Expert	5	19	8
Star	6	19	5
Director	7	19	4
Friend	8	18	4
Spirit	9	17	5
PMA Score	49%		
Cluster Importance			
Relationship (R)	32%		
Achievement (A)	34%		
Growth (G)	34%		

Figure 7.6 Alan's second Motivational Map

motivator but full satisfied (10/10) has now become his sixth motivator, but interestingly is only 5/10. In other words, Alan's motivational world has been turned upside down by his experiences at AHDSP over the last 6 months!

And to cap this, third, his cluster (RAG) importance has changed:[7]

Relationship motivators are 3% lower
Achievement motivators are 8% higher
Growth motivators are 5% lower

This seemingly may be a good thing, because Jane did observe that the original Map with Alan did raise the prospect of the 'idealistic friend', as she put it, who would not be able to achieve much. When faced with two radically different Maps like this – over such a short time frame – one has to question not the veracity of the Maps (for they are 'true' at the point of completion) but which motivators are really home base for Alan. In other words, the pressure he is now under is affecting his core beliefs,[8] and these beliefs are changing his motivational profile; but is it sustainable? Is Alan 'forcing' himself to undertake activities against his own motivational 'grain', as it were, and is this forcing him to adopt beliefs that are not really his?

On the other hand, the cluster (RAG) is reflective of a change of motivators for Alan, which could or may be positive for the organisation in terms of the practical achievements, especially regarding the financial aspects for the company, where Builder could be powerfully useful. That said, his shift in motivators does not seem to bode well for the key areas of development for Alan, building a team and individual relationships. Note the Director motivator is low in both Maps, but in the second his satisfaction with his own sense of control – that is, management – is only 4/10.

We have a lot, then, from the Maps to base our forward-thinking about Alan on. Jane knew at this point that doing a Motivational 360° Team feedback from his colleagues on Alan would be very powerful indeed, and possibly one of the few things that might save his career. The benefits of providing such an in-depth view of Alan would enable him to:

- better assess his own behaviours, communication skills and personal impact
- identify if the improvement in delivering his KPIs was damaging his relationships with his colleagues, thereby disengaging fellow team members
- identify specific ways to strengthen these relationships, and improve his relationship-building, influencing and engagement skills.

To this end Alan's staff were sent a carefully worded email from Jane Thomas.

We reproduce this email because it is important to see what we are asking other employees[9] and leaders to do; this is not as straightforward as simply

Hello everyone,

I am aware that you have been informed that as part of Alan's appraisal and performance review feedback from you would be extremely valuable. When the feedback is given to Alan you will not be identified, only Jane Thomas and the CEO need to know who gave the feedback. Please put your name on the questionnaire.

We want you to give YOUR perceptions of Alan. We are NOT asking you to try and predict how you think Alan might respond; instead, we want you to focus on what he does and says based on what you know of Alan. Based on your interactions with him, what do you feel, out of the two statements offered, best represents what would be Alan's preferences or priorities? How strongly do you feel each statement would need to be to accurately reflect Alan's Leadership style and approach?

When you complete the questionnaire please remember the 'I want' or 'I feel' statements are about how you see Alan... NOT ABOUT YOU ... replace I with Alan i.e. Alan wants or feels etc. Look at both statements. Would you say Alan has a preference or do you think both statements are applicable? If you feel both apply you will score more in the centre, if a statement is stronger you will score him towards the left or right of that statement.

Please remember you are completing the map on Alan as you see him. Thank you and much appreciated.

Figure 7.7 Jane Thomas' email to Alan's staff

asking someone to do a Map. Clearly, this is highly subjective, which sounds like a negative, but actually is an extreme positive when we think about it: we have here the 'perceptions' of what staff feel motivates Alan AND, critically, we know from Alan's Motivational Map what actually does. Effectively, we are going to get a Map that establishes how Alan 'comes across' to his fellow employees; whether their perceptions are right or wrong, they are what they are, and they are what the true leader must always deal with, and it is the starting point of all leadership effectiveness. As Dr Alan Watkins expressed[10] it,

> Coherent Enlightened Leaders will therefore not only recognise that the troops are in an emotionally different place from them, which is itself a skill, but will have sufficient emotional flexibility to offer different emotional input depending on where the team is on the roller-coaster of change.

Alan's employee Motivational 360° Team Map came out like this (Alan's Map being his second one in Figure 7.6).

Activity 7.5

Alan was given feedback on this Map by Jane Thomas, the consultant, along with the CEO. What are some key points that this Figure 7.8 reveals? As you look at the numbers, don't forget to go back to Figure 7.6 to see what Alan's

Name	Director	Spirit	Creator	Searcher	Expert	Star	Builder	Defender	Friend	Personal Motivation	1	2	3
Alan	19	17	22	23	19	19	24	19	18	49%	3	8	7
OM	34	33	22	14	20	19	19	18	1	76%	8	8	4
SE	26	21	20	23	24	13	14	24	15	52%	3	9	7
E1	35	30	18	12	18	25	18	13	11	12%	1	1	3
SM	23	24	18	10	25	30	14	18	18	76%	9	4	10
A1	29	26	18	19	22	23	19	14	10	99%	10	10	9
E2	28	26	29	18	14	26	17	10	12	61%	6	6	7
A2	20	22	22	31	17	16	19	15	18	67%	7	6	7
A3	20	20	20	29	23	12	16	23	17	90%	9	9	9
A4	15	22	18	24	20	17	20	25	19	89%	9	9	8
Total	249	241	207	203	202	200	180	179	139	67%			

Figure 7.8 Alan's employee Motivational 360° Team Map

Key: Dark grey – 1st motivator, middle grey – 2nd motivator, light grey – 3rd motivator, textured grey – lowest motivator

actual motivational profile is. Remember too that Figure 7.6 represents Alan's most recent profile; Figure 7.1 shows his original motivators.

The first thing, perhaps, to notice in this 360° Map is that whereas Alan is actually 49% motivated, staff see him as being more motivated than that: 67% motivated. This is good in so far as the leader does need to be perceived as being highly motivated, but 67% is only in the Boost Zone,[11] whereas in reality Alan needs to be in the Optimal Zone (of 80%+), where he was originally. Moreover, there is a serious further issue with this score: we expect different members of staff to see Alan 'differently', but the range of differences here is very extreme. At the top end staff member A1 sees him as 99% motivated, whereas at the bottom end, engineer E1, he is only 12% motivated! That is a difference of 87 points. If motivation were something 'objective' how could that be? The possible inference we might make from this is that Alan is treating different people very differently, and because he is doing so, a perception of unfairness has arisen which is distorting perceptions of him – both ways in fact: the 'favourites' and the less favoured.

Second, nobody perceived what Alan's top motivator is, The Builder; his second motivator, The Searcher, only three out of the nine staff identified as in his top three; which means that only The Creator, his third motivator, was rightly identified as being his third motivator. In short, the staff have little idea of what is really driving Alan, and if they were to base their actions on what they think is motivating him, then they would be wrong.

Third, and perhaps most important of all, the two motivators they do identify as revealing his behaviours, are in fact his lowest and ante-penultimate lowest motivators, the Spirit and the Director. This is especially interesting because both these motivators, we can be very sure, are not real motivators for Alan. We know this because in his first Map, Figure 7.1, both these motivators are still low (fifth and sixth respectively). Thus, two more issues arise from this: first, that it is almost certain that the employees see Alan as wholly inconsistent in his behaviours. How do we know this? Because he is exercising control, The Director, and at the same time exercising freedom, probably for himself, which means he is not following the rules he himself lays out. Second, all The Director scores, bar Alan's own (19/40) and admin A4 (15/40), are 20 and above, and furthermore those five who have identified Director as being in Alan's top three have done so with extremely high scores: 34, 26, 35, 29, and 28. This is way above average, suggesting that Alan is seriously 'controlling' these people in his efforts to get results. Notice it is the two senior people especially, that is, those with whom Alan would have most interaction, whose scores are most 'spikey'.[12] And also notice that three of the people who have identified Alan as a Director have also identified him as Friend lowest – look at the Office Manager's (OM) scoring. One senses that with Alan's Director at 34/40 and his Friend at 1/40 the Office Manager really doesn't like Alan one little bit.

There is so much more in these numbers that Jane obviously did draw out in the sessions she had, but for now we need to summarise what we have found in order to begin the process of creating an action plan to help Alan. What points, then, must feed this action plan?1
That staff do not understand his behaviours and 'where he is coming from'
2   That he is demotivating and disengaging staff by his actions
3   That he needs to 'refresh' his own motivators and be sure what those motivators are
4   That 'controlling' staff is not efficacious, is sub-optimal at best, that new leadership and team skills and approaches are necessary
5   That results derive from the synergy of teams: relationships at work are highly important and all things associated with them such as collaboration, inclusivity and helping people feel valued; all key drivers of employee engagement.

If these issues could be addressed, Alan may be able to help get the business back on track, as well as getting his career back on track too! So rather than Alan 'directing' his staff he is going to need to consciously adjust his behaviour and style to suit his colleagues. And not just his staff: what about his own bosses, the leaders on the Board to whom he is answerable? What do they see when they look at Alan's behaviour? Do they see what the staff see? This is a really fascinating question because in a person who was behaving consistently we might expect the answer to be yes: they would see the same person because the behaviours would be similar.

Activity 7.6

A very simple activity here. Simply predict yes or no: do you think that Alan's 360° Motivational Team Map from his leadership team will provide a comparable map to the one the staff generated in Figure 7.8? Whatever your answer, jot down reasons for it.

Activity 7.7

Study the Map in Figure 7.9. Identify three key points that it reveals about Alan and his work. It clearly is very different from the staff map in Figure 7.8. What comments might you make about these differences?

Clearly, the senior management has an altogether different perspective on the motivators of Alan, if not on his levels of motivation. So the impression he creates in terms of his activities is that he is (for both senior leaders and the staff) somewhere in the mid-60% for his motivational scoring, nearly some 20% above what he actually feels at 49%. But the big issue is that the senior leadership see Alan as driven by Star-Searcher-Director whereas the staff see Alan as driven by Director-Spirit-Creator. The one common element of The

Name	Star	Searcher	Director	Creator	Expert	Builder	Spirit	Friend	Defender	Personal Motivation	1	2	3
Alan	19	23	19	22	19	24	17	18	19	49%	3	8	7
CEO	28	23	32	21	19	12	14	18	13	41%	3	5	8
SALES D	28	28	17	15	19	20	16	17	20	89%	10	8	5
OPS D	28	23	24	27	22	10	16	21	9	79%	8	8	7
SERVICE D	25	17	21	19	20	25	27	7	19	64%	7	5	7
Total	128	114	113	104	99	91	90	81	80	64%			

Figure 7.9 Senior leadership Motivational 360° Team Map
Key: Dark grey – 1st motivator, middle grey – 2nd motivator, light grey – 3rd motivator, textured grey – lowest motivator

Director might be perceived as being a positive in that we want leaders to want to take control, but given what we already know from our analysis of Figure 7.8, we have to ask: is this really a positive or merely the observation that Alan likes to be in charge and possibly throw his weight around – less so with the senior people of course (hence only third in their ranking), but definitely so with the staff.

Further, this suggestion that Alan may not be effectively 'controlling' his staff is reinforced by the most important score of all: the CEO's! He sees Director as Alan's number 1 motivator at 32/40, so a real spike, but notice that he scores the satisfaction rating as 3/10. The CEO as the commander in chief has worked most closely with Alan, and so his rating Alan, as Alan, in this way can only suggest that as a leader the little satisfaction (3/10) that Alan is deriving from his work must imply failure so far in his leadership role with the staff. If we go back to Figure 7.6 we find that Alan's own satisfaction rating with the Director motivator is 4/10, which means the CEO is uncannily accurate. Keep in mind too just how specific this is: the CEO is clearly not just 'rubbishing' Alan; he is trying to see him through the motivational perspective. So that, for example, if we look at the CEO's evaluation of Alan's third motivator in Figure 7.9, we see that the Searcher is scored 8/10 by the CEO – and lo! Alan scores himself 8/10 for this motivator too. Thus, Alan is almost certainly making a difference, and this we established in his first review with Jane Thomas when we considered Figure 7.3 and Alan's positives; but as we noted then, the positives all tend to be discrete tasks, the overt and 'thing' stuff; whereas all the soft skill and true leadership capabilities, the human and ambiguous developmental components, were more or less completely deficient.

This leads on to, perhaps, a root problem that Alan has and is unaware of himself: namely, all four directors see Alan as having Star motivation either as first or second motivator. In both Maps that he completed Alan's Star motivator is low (in Figure 7.1 ranking eighth, and in Figure 7.6 ranking sixth). How could all four leaders of the company see something completely not in Alan's profile – and staff collectively only rank it sixth, though four employees do see this in their top three for Alan – and rank it so highly, pre-eminent in fact? What does this mean? What does this suggest?

It suggests, first, that Alan behaves differently with senior staff than with subordinates; and the thing it most suggests is that Alan is striving to gain recognition, more accurately, to impress his seniors and is seeking to curry favour with them. He is less bothered about seeking favour with his juniors. To add to this, we also need to observe the following: all motivators are equal, but everything in the world of motivation is contextual. So it is entirely possible to say a particular motivator is less good, less optimum, less ideal in a given context. Now the context that Alan is in requires the building of strong teams: if the dominant motivator is Star for the leader of that team, then there may be a dangerous tendency which leads to the leader failing to give credit to the team as the leader seeks to acquire or accrue it to them-selves;[13] in this way team morale and motivation and cohesion is undermined.

Before seeing Alan about these results and having a conversation about management styles, Jane thought it would be helpful to pull them altogether into one 360° Motivational Team Map. This was because Jane thought it better –without losing the insights of the separate 360° Maps – to try to get Alan to respond holistically to one set of results which he could contrast with his own actual Map.

Pulling the Directors and staff 360° feedback together, we have Figure 7.10.

Activity 7.8

We now have the final 360° Motivational Team Map showing how all the key senior and junior employees in the company view Alan. What three key points do you observe from this? And why are they significant? What would you do on the basis on these motivational perceptions?

Probably the single most important observation to make about this Map is to point out that the staff collectively have entirely failed to grasp what Alan's top three motivators actually are! Put another way, Alan has entirely failed, and not deliberately in this case (that is, he is unaware of what he behaviours are conveying about himself), to reveal what it is he wants and what is important to him. This is a failure of communication at a deeper level than merely saying he fails to communicate effectively; usually, what we mean by failing to communicate effectively is either that the goals or objectives are unclear or mixed, or that the forms of expression used are ambiguous or cloudy. Here, however, because motivation drives behaviour, what we have is

Name	Director	Spirit	Star	Searcher	Creator	Expert	Builder	Defender	Friend	Motivation Audit	1	2	3
Alan	19	17	19	23	22	19	24	19	18	49%	3	8	7
CEO	32	14	28	23	21	19	12	13	18	41%	3	5	8
OM	34	33	19	14	22	20	19	18	1	76%	8	8	4
SALES D	17	16	28	28	15	19	20	20	17	89%	10	8	5
OPS D	24	16	28	23	27	22	10	9	21	79%	8	8	7
SE	26	21	13	23	20	24	14	24	15	52%	3	9	7
E1	35	30	25	12	18	18	18	13	11	12%	1	1	3
SM	23	24	30	10	18	25	14	18	18	76%	9	4	10
A1f	29	26	23	19	18	22	19	14	10	99%	10	10	9
E2	28	26	26	18	29	14	17	10	12	61%	6	6	7
A2	20	22	16	31	22	17	19	15	18	67%	7	6	7
A3f	20	20	12	29	20	23	16	23	17	90%	9	9	9
A4	15	22	17	24	18	20	20	25	19	89%	9	9	8
SERVICE D	21	27	25	17	19	20	25	19	7	64%	7	5	7
Total	343	314	309	294	289	282	247	240	202	67%			

Figure 7.10 Senior leadership and staff combined motivational 360° Team Map

Key: Dark grey – 1st motivator, middle grey – 2nd motivator, light grey – 3rd motivator, textured grey – lowest motivator

someone coming across as completely inauthentic, insincere, unaware and, at best, confused in their whole approach to what they are doing in leading employees, as well as interacting with senior staff.

Second, that the perceptions are very extreme. We see this in a number of ways. Most obviously in the range of scoring: from 99% to 12%; from Audit scores from 10 to 1; but less obviously, but equally importantly, we find that even at the top end of the motivators there is at least one person who sees it as Alan's lowest, including himself with the Spirit. This last point is very unusual, and it points towards inconsistency of conduct.

Third – and to be very clear here, there is so much more than just three points! – we need to address which motivator or motivators are most problematic in this puzzle of Alan's failure with his staff and with his own senior team. This obviously is a tricky issue: for example, the Spirit and Star motivators both being perceived as within his top three can cause problems when their negative or downside is operational. In the case of the Spirit it can lead to the perception of non-accountability; in the case of the Star, it can lead to the sense of competing with one's team, or even of being above them. But Jane concluded, rightly, that the big issue here was the number 1 motivator: The Director, but not just because it was number 1, but because it was not alone. For Director highest with Friend lowest is what we call a 'polarity reinforcement'.[14]

Crucially, what is happening here is the following: Alan is perceived simultaneously as 'controlling' whilst at the same time as being perceived as not belonging, not a team player, or even positively unfriendly; in other words, dislikeable. Notice with the scoring: that Star (third with 309 points) and Spirit (second with 314 points) are closely scored; there is not much between their scoring. But Director at 343 points is way ahead of the second and third perceived motivators. Equally, at the other end, we have Builder and Defender (seventh and eighth ranked in importance) closely scored at 247 and 240 respectively; but then Friend drops off a cliff, as it were, with only 202 points. The point being: we can put up, sometimes, with people who control us if we like them; but it becomes intolerable if we don't. What we have here is a command and control style of leadership that colleagues perceive Alan practises, rather than the mind-set of High Challenge, High Support we talked about in Figure 7.2.

Remember, Alan had rated himself as High Challenge and High Support, but what the maps are showing very clearly is that he is High Challenge and Low Support, and so driving staff in the 'Stress' quadrant.

And, despite the initial inputs from Jane to Alan, he was no further forward; Jane and the CEO could clearly see the danger looming ahead if this situation was allowed to go un-remedied. Staff would inevitably revenge themselves on Alan, usually through passive aggression: sabotaging surreptitiously his ideas, his orders, and his efforts. But what to do about it?

Alan's actual Map (Figure 7.6) showed Relationships were his weakest motivators; yet in his first Map (Figure 7.1) they were not. Achievement motivators were lowest. It's as if Alan has seesawed from one extreme to another. In his first Map relationships (Friend was second) were important to him, but it's as if he had to harden himself, ramp up his achievement drives, and in the process lose sight of the importance of relationships to him. He has been unable to balance both things – relationships and achievement – at the same time.

Jane's initial suspicions about the suitability of Alan as a senior leader within AHDSP were now fully realised. The evidence was all in and it pointed towards one unmistakeable fact:[15] that Alan, despite an impressive CV and a good, talked-up story, had chronically low levels of self-esteem.[16] He hid it well, though his earlier tendency to blame others was a warning, and much of his work at work was not about the 'work', but about concealing his own feelings of inferiority and inefficacy. If you will, like a child who shouts loud in the dark to disguise the fact of their underlying fear. Alan had played his 'game', but now the evidence was in. Was it, therefore, wise to try to develop Alan further? Would skills training be effective in a case where low self-esteem was the real issue?

This was the issue that Jane took to the CEO with another and new insight into the Maps. There is a point at which the Map is accurate but irrelevant to outcomes. This occurs in a small percentage of the population when they go below what in Maslow's terms are the security drives[17] and seek only to satisfy their physiological needs. The 'drives' are what we want, but the physiological needs are just that, needs based on the need to survive. People at this level may 'want' things – their motivators – but their needs always trump their wants. They invariably develop a certain cunning in seeming to supply what others 'want', but in reality servicing what they 'need'. In other words, they become like chameleons, adopting to their environment, and they play 'games',[18] which becomes apparent from their inconsistencies. Their only actual consistency is their ego-consistency to satisfy themselves.

The extreme variation in Alan's own Maps in Figures 7.1 and 7.6 was perhaps the first indication of an instability, a lack of rootedness and consistency, that might indicate chronically low self-esteem, despite all the bluster to the contrary. The massive variations in perception in the two (and the third combined) Motivational 360° Team Maps further reinforced this sense of disconnect between who Alan was and who the staff and management perceived him to be – keep in mind, just how extreme this was. And finally, in the feedback of the 360° Team Map results to Alan there seemed to be no real embracing of what the results were showing: from Alan's perspective there was a mismatch between the CEO's preferred rate of change (slow) and his own (fast), and the question was simply that staff needed more 'performance management systems' to get up to speed. But the CEO had realised the necessary support needed, hence the 360° feedback as well as the coaching from Jane around the objectives in Figure 7.5. On these objectives, however, Alan was totally non-receptive; it appeared that Alan would either be like a bull in a china shop, attacking any problem, or would be entirely risk-averse and timid. There was no consistency in his approach; hence the confused staff.

Further, Jane thought that although Alan knew all about Motivational Maps, had an actual Team Map of his staff, and knew how to link this to reward strategies, he wasn't really using this at all – possibly, in his own mind, because he knew 'better' or because he was non-receptive to this requirement of his job, and so could not change his behaviour.

Jane's view was: the CEO should find reasons to release Alan as he was never going to succeed in the long-term. Certain 'hard' issues had been addressed by Alan, for which thanks, but now he needed to be replaced by a leader who could lead the staff and motivate them. The CEO agreed; so began the HR process that is outside the scope of this book, but suffice to say Alan was supported, but released within 3 months. It was impossible for him to stay without jeopardising the whole business. But using Motivational 360° Team Maps had flagged up very early on the acute problem, indeed threat to the business, that Alan – unaware even to himself even – posed.

Away from this tricky situation, our final chapter looks at the last ingredient of the '4+1' model: leading to motivate employees. What Alan should have understood and done?

Notes

1 James Sale and Bevis Moynan, *Mapping Motivation for Coaching*, Routledge (2018) and James Sale and Steve Jones, *Mapping Motivation for Engagement*, Routledge (2018).

2 Lou Adler, a world expert on recruitment, has much to say on all the ideas in this paragraph. See: *Hire with Your Head: A Rational Way to Make a Gut Reaction* (1998)

3 Being fully aware, of course, that becoming too 'friendly' as a leader can also sabotage one's personal authority as well as compromising one's ability to take 'difficult' decisions.

4 This is covered in some detail in *Mapping Motivation for Engagement*, ibid., Chapter 4.

5 "… part of the issue is the leader's willingness to scrutinise their own behaviour as hard as they do of other people" – George Binney and Colin Williams, *Leaning into the Future*, Nicolas Brealey (1995).

6 For a full account of the 4 Zones see *Mapping Motivation*, James Sale, Routledge (2016), Chapter 4.

7 Notice too how the range of scores has narrowed: from 16 (29–13) in Figure 7.1 to 7 (24–17) in Figure 7.6. This is highly significant: the 'spike' that Alan had in his motivational profile has become blunted into a more amorphous melting pot. Being more 'balanced' here is probably not as helpful as it might appear to be.

8 Again, for more on how beliefs within the self-concept and of expectations affect motivators, see *Mapping Motivation*, ibid., Chapter 2. The personality, too, which

is 'fixed' has a part to play in the motivational profile, so it can be the case that the motivations change under duress, but some part – from the personality – wants to reassert itself.

9 See Figure 3.4 for a variant set of instructions in completing the Motivational 360° Team Map.

10 Dr Alan Watkins, *Coherence*, Kogan Page (2014).

11 See endnote 4 above for more on the motivational Zones.

12 Scores of 30 or above are called 'spikes' and represent not just a motivator, but an intense desire; conversely, scores of 10 or less are called 'inverse spikes' and represent a motivator fading away to perhaps become an intense aversion.

13 The opposite of this is advocated in so many texts, ancient and modern. But consider Lao Tzu, "When the best leader's work is done the people say, 'We did it ourselves' or 'If a wholly Great One rules the people hardly know that he exists" – Lao Tzu, *Tao Te Ching*, 17, Richard Wilhelm edition.

14 For more on polarity reinforcement, see *Mapping Motivation*, ibid., Chapter 4, and *Mapping Motivation for Coaching*, ibid., Chapter 6. Essentially, polarity reinforcement is where two motivators of opposing drive are not conflicting with each other because they are in the top 3 together, but 1 is top and 1 is lowest. Clearly, since the lowest opposes the top, then by being low it actually reinforces the strength of the top since it is not available to counter the top motivator.

15 Writing in *The 33 Strategies of War*, Profile Books (2006), Robert Greene writes: "People's personalities often form around weaknesses, character flaws, uncontrollable emotions. People who feel needy, or who have a superiority complex, or are afraid of chaos, or desperately want order, will develop a personality – a social mask – to cover up their flaws and make it possible for them to present a confident, pleasant, responsible exterior to the world". This, in a nutshell, is what Jane has discovered using the Maps about Alan.

16 For much more on building strong self-esteem and several tools to help on this, see *Mapping Motivation for Coaching*, ibid. Also, one of the world's leading experts on self-esteem: Dr Nathaniel Brandon, *The Psychology of High Self-Esteem*, Nightingale Conant (1986).

17 For more on Maslow's *Hierarchy of Needs*, see *Mapping Motivation*, ibid., Chapter 3 and especially Figure 3.3.

18 The classic book on this is Thomas A Harris, *I'm OK, You're OK: A Practical Guide to Transactional Analysis*, Harper & Row (1969).

Chapter 8

Leading to motivate employees

Finally, we come to the final element of the '4+1' model: namely, the leader needs to motivate[1] those for whom they have direct line responsibility; and if they are senior, then to plan for their influence to motivate all employees within an organisation, given that there will be many with whom they do not come into direct contact. Nevertheless, as leaders we are being watched, studied, observed all the time, and everything we do counts. Either, people are deciding that we are trustworthy, competent and motivated, so that they want to follow us, or they are concluding that we are untrustworthy, incompetent and de-motivated and de-motivating, and they were wishing they had somebody else as a leader, or that they were somewhere else.

In a sense, all we have been talking about so far impacts on the individual's motivation. We know from all the literature to that effect that the thinking, doing and team building all are necessary components in the employees' mind to support their decision to want to follow the leader. If no 'thinking' – no vision, no strategy – has been done, then clearly the organisation will ricochet like a pinball on a game machine, instead of making progress to some real and meaningful goals. If there is no 'doing' – then there will be no implementation of plans, no clear roles, no action; just talk, and more talk, and a dispiriting idleness or lethargy. If there is no 'team work', then there will be the ongoing de-motivation of individual against individual, department competing against department, all supposedly being on the same side! How bad would that be?

And, considering the '+1' element of the model, if the leader did not keep themselves constantly fresh, informed, and well-equipped and trained, then staff would lose confidence in their ultimate efficacy; the joy of work would turn into the routine of work, and alongside that a business as usual mind-set would develop that is so destructive of true engagement. That, of course, would lead to organisational failure; as Sun Tzu noted,[2] "competitive success ... is determined by leadership skill alone" and "Leaders who complain about morale of their employees evidently do not realise that employee's morale is a mirror of confidence in their leadership".

All these aspects, therefore, impact the employees' motivation. There are hundreds of books already on the need for leaders to be integrous, to walk the talk, to be consistent, to be up-skilled and effective, and every one of these things does contribute to motivation and staff engagement. We have to take these as givens here, for as John Adair[3] noted: "Without respect, leadership is fatally impaired".[4] So we are not going to pretend that just thinking about motivation, mapping motivation, without reference to these wider, ethical issues of behaviour would magically solve all motivational problems. But what we want to consider is motivation per se; in other words, given the walk-the-talk, value-positive approach of a true leader, then what else might the leader do motivationally, specifically motivationally, and in order to optimise employee motivation, including their own?

We make this last point – the leader needs to optimise their own motivation – because we often say that the leader's own motivation is a barometer for everyone else's. How can the leader expect others to be highly motivated if it is palpably obvious that they themselves are not?[5] So, as we think about the employee and the individual, we need to consider what will fortify and increase the leader's own motivation.

Activity 8.1

Review how you increase your own motivation. What typically do you do? How often do you do it, and is there a plan for ongoing motivational re-energisation? If not, what plan do you have to ensure you are always as motivated as possible?

Activity 8.2

The first thing to do in order to be as fully motivated as your environment can allow is to do a Motivational Map and study its proposed Reward Strategies. If you have not done one, go to endnote 21 of the Preface to this book to find out how to access a Map. Once you have done the Motivational Map, especially study pages 7–9 of it, which provide specific reward strategies based on your top three motivators. Ask yourself, which of these might be beneficial and applicable to my situation? Also, consider page 10 of your Map, which gives important information about your lowest motivator and its implications. Remember, your lowest motivator,[6] because it seems to be, or 'feels' to be, not emotionally important, can become your own Achilles' Heel. Use the M.A. P. – the Motivational Action Plan – on page 14 of your Map to commit to taking action.

But thinking about Activity 8.2 and mentioning the 'Achilles' Heel' of a motivational profile leads on to a consideration of the wider issue of strengths and weaknesses, motivationally speaking. We are all familiar with a SWOT[7] analysis: that is, considering the Strengths, Weaknesses, Opportunities and

Threats posed by an analysis of any situation and our resources in relationship to that situation. Well, the Motivational Maps enable us to do a Motivational Maps SWOT analysis. What is, then, a Motivational Maps' SWOT analysis? It is a way of considering what some of the issues might be for an individual, team, or organisational based on the specific motivators that emerge from the two opposing polarities of Strength versus Weakness, and Opportunity versus Threat.

If we look at Figure 8.1 we see a SWOT analysis based on the three Growth Motivators at the apex of the Maslow Hierarchy.[8] It would be too long-winded to go through what this means for all nine motivators, but we will outline what we see as its significance for the Searcher[9] motivator.

Thus, we see that the Strengths that the Searcher brings to any situation are: the intense desire to find out why they are doing what they are doing, and to have a meaningful reason(s) for their activities. How is that a Strength? It is valuable to an organisation because at root it identifies value and values. That can be important in identifying what the organisation stands for; equally importantly, it can help the organisation serve the customer or client more effectively, because it leads to understanding more fully what the customer really wants.

Alongside this, the Searcher's Strength is also in the desire for constructive feedback. Note: this isn't just praise. Constructive feedback is the essence of the ability to improve one's performance; and also to 'course correct'. In

MOTIVATOR	STRENGTHS	WEAKNESSES	OPPORTUNITIES	THREATS
SEARCHER	Asks why? Values feedback Makes a difference	Unlikely to ask 'why not' Easily bored by mundane details Intolerant of others values	Achieve higher purpose Cope with complexity Transform/ improve a specific 'domain'	Meaninglessness/ pointlessness Over extension Insufficient mentoring and evaluation
SPIRIT	Independence Decisiveness Thinking differently	Distant Non-synergistic Poor management	Exploratory/ opportunistic Contrarian positions Empowerment	Isolation/ no-alliances Failure to consult/ consolidate Reckless
CREATOR	Solves problems Innovates Original viewpoints	Impatience Restlessness Frustration with status quo	Researching solutions Complex issues Realising potential	Business as usual Repetitive operations Lack of change

Figure 8.1 SWOT for the Growth Motivators

other words, to respond effectively to circumstances and take appropriate action. This means that Searchers tend to bring a certain openness and flexibility to any situation.

Finally, the Searcher's Strength is all about making a difference: they drive change, they want change, and results are as important to them, perhaps more so, than to any other motivator with the possible exception of the Builder. Is that a Strength? We think so: this is someone driven by making a difference and achieving specific outcomes, a major asset for any organisation.

But on the other side, the Weaknesses are significant too: just as they are likely to want to know why, they are less likely, particularly when they are persuaded of the value or rightness of some activity, to ask 'why not'? This can lead to an unrealistic idealism, to unremitting work and burnout, and also to a failure to appreciate the importance of proper process for generating systems. This is, of course, because creating a 'proper process' is slow and time-consuming, whereas the Searcher tends to want to act quickly.

And this leads on to their tendency to be bored – and so skip – mundane details: the big picture obsesses them and they can be blind to the small things that are either important to the success of the venture, or to the people the leader is leading. It's all very well getting excited about climbing Everest, but the team will certainly want someone to have considered packing 'sandwiches' in their back pack!

Last, because the Searcher tends to be a 'believer' in causes, or a specific cause, it can become easy to be intolerant of others' values, and this is dangerous for teamwork and also for the motivations of the individual. Indeed, without even realising it, the Searcher leader may recruit and seek others with the same motivational profile and beliefs as themselves, and not see that it is not necessarily the best balance. Being tolerant of others is important, as is weeding out the incompetent.[10]

So, the Opportunities that Searcher types bring to the organisation are very specific: they look for a higher purpose and to realise it; they will wrestle with complexity and complex problems in order to make a difference; and they wish to transform, or at least improve, a particular 'domain' or 'field' that they are working in. Another way of putting this might be: the opportunities for Searchers range from bringing about break-through innovations to developing higher levels of quality in any service or product.

The downside, though, or threats, are real enough: any leader considering a Searcher individual or team needs to be aware that meaninglessness or pointlessness in the work is going to be seriously demotivating, and will crash performance after a while – it is only a matter of time. Leaders, then, have to ask themselves: how meaningful is the work, and how can I enrich[11] it if the leader concludes it is entirely routine?

Also, as a threat, and picking up on the 'unrealistic idealism' we mentioned with potential weaknesses, we have the possibility of the Searcher overextending themselves. On the one hand, this can lead to burnout, as we have observed, but on the other there is another dangerous implication. We see this most forcefully, perhaps, in the caring professions (but too in management anywhere!), often employing Searcher-driven individuals: priests or teachers or social workers and the like – wholly committed – who not only burnout, but who become ineffective too. This is because they have over-extended themselves, taken on too many projects, become responsible for too many people and objectives, and no *one* task is ultimately done well. It is the opposite of focus; instead, there is a dissipation of energies.

One final weakness to comment on would be the tendency of the idealistic, value-driven, make-a-difference motivational type to underestimate the knowledge, skills and resilience that they are going to require to successfully deliver the mission. Enthusiasm counts for much; as does motivation, which is after all energy. But as we know, strong motivation, whilst a decisive factor – as are powerful values and ideals – does not account for all the performance mix[12]. Thus, there is a need to mentor and coach the Searcher to ensure – via evaluation – that they are on track. Searchers are highly receptive to learning because, considered properly, it self-evidently helps realise the mission by equipping and upskilling the employee or the leader. But it is all too easy to lose sight of its necessity in the Searcher's enthusiasm and excitement for changing the world or making that difference.

From the leader's perspective, then, we have a series of motivational SWOT questions and issues to consider when we look at our people and teams

Activity 8.3

Look at Figure 8.1 and choose either the Spirit or Creator motivator. Expand your understanding of what SWOT might mean for your chosen motivator. For example, if you are working with the Spirit, ask for Strengths, how 'independence' might be an asset? Or, for Weaknesses, how being 'distant' might prove a problem, and so on. Whenever you see an individual or team map, run through the implications of the SWOT. The SWOTs for the Achievement and Relationship Motivators are below in Figures 8.2 and 8.3.

Using the motivational SWOT, we think, will help the leader fortify and increase their own motivation because they are extending their knowledge and potential 'control' (here meant in an entirely positive way, as in the ability to influence the course of events through people) over their own and their employees' motivations. This will impact their energy, their self-esteem, and their competence or skill level.

So, we have the leader reading their own Map to increase their motivation; we also have their using the motivational SWOT to help understand motivational issues within a given context. A third way of fortifying motivation for the leader is understanding what we call the People/Thing issue! We are looking for leaders who can motivate but also motivate beyond the moment – beyond just the short-term. Indeed, short-termism[13] is a chronic problem long recognised by all serious commentators on organisational life.

MOTIVATOR	STRENGTHS	WEAKNESSES	OPPORTUNITIES	THREATS
EXPERT	Knowledgeable Master skill set Learning focus	Pedantry Small picture thinking Arrogant	Superior products/ services Advanced know-how Competitive advantage	Know-it-all mentality Change-aversion Lack of perspective
BUILDER	Competitive Results orientation Bottom-line thinking	Lack of higher purpose Team disruptor Self-centred	Building commercial operations Opportunism Making deals/ negotiation	Single monetary focus, so blind spots Lack of systems/ process Weak alliances
DIRECTOR	Leadership Direction Involvement	Micro-management Autocracy Disempowerment	Optimising resources Clarity Delivery	Conflicts/friction Egos/other Directors Failure to consult

Figure 8.2 SWOT for the Achievement Motivators

MOTIVATOR	STRENGTHS	WEAKNESSES	OPPORTUNITIES	THREATS
STAR	Marketing Positioning Highlighting what is good	Needy for recognition Not acknowledging others' contributions Failure to see wider organisational issues	Raising profile High impact Networking	Other Stars/ over competitive Disconnection from others Inciting envy in others
FRIEND	Collaborative Team player Loyalty	Work/operate in isolation Too relationship dependent Minimal challenge	Stabilising new team projects Long-term team projects Trust situations	Impersonal, friendless environments 'Heavy' management Non-consistent communications
DEFENDER	Methodical Reliable Process-driven	Risk/change averse Inflexible Slow	Ensuring the basics are right Stabilising volatile situations Creating efficiences	Poor planning/ plans Lack of time Unfair or confusing situations

Figure 8.3 SWOT for the Relationship Motivators

Activity 8.4

Try completing these two sentences:

1   The most difficult thing to deal with in any business or any organisation is …
2   The most difficult thing to deal with in life is …

Write down your answer to these two questions and before you do, take time to review your own experience of business or organisational life, as well as considering your own life to ask what has caused you the most problems.

There can be no one right answer for everyone, but we have found that when people reflect on it one answer represents over 90% of everyone's answer! And we think, too, that if the less than 10% who don't give this answer were critically interrogated, then they also would agree with the 90%. Namely, the most difficult thing about being or working in any organisation is the people; other people are always the problem;[14] usually fellow employees and bosses, but sometimes customers and clients; but people. In one's own life, the same is also true: other people cause us problems, and this goes right back to parenting and teachers; and this can lead to situations where the person who is the problem in our own life is … ME. I am the person who is my own problem; and I constantly self-sabotage my own welfare and progress, largely through the erroneous and false limiting beliefs[15] that I have adopted as my own.

The implications of this are profound for leadership; for it is as if we imbibe a mind-set that is inimical to real leadership, and especially to true motivation, as a result of our almost innate knowledge or feeling that people are the problem. And it leads most people, including leaders, to make the first fatal mistake in their tenure as leaders. Keep in mind, of course, that we are all called to lead in or at something even if we are not technically leaders in the work space.

The key thing leaders must understand and resist in their own beliefs is simply this: people are not 'things'. There, we have said it: a person is not a thing. It sounds so obvious, but it is not. It leads to three problems that leaders[16] have:

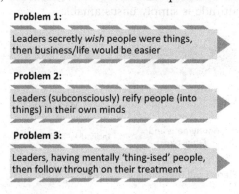

Problem 1:

Leaders secretly *wish* people were things, then business/life would be easier

Problem 2:

Leaders (subconsciously) reify people (into things) in their own minds

Problem 3:

Leaders, having mentally 'thing-ised' people, then follow through on their treatment

Figure 8.4 Three problems leaders have

Activity 8.5

Consider the three problems we have outlined in Figure 8.4. Why do leaders secretly wish people were things? What is the effect of reifying[17] people? And what might the 'follow through' look like in general terms?

To understand why leaders (and to be fair, people generally) wish that people were things requires us to explore – as banal perhaps as it seems – the difference between a person and a thing. In other words, we have to ask another, a deeper question.

Activity 8.6

In your opinion, list the differences between people and things. Which of these differences are truly significant for leadership?

Let's consider these three core distinctions we are making in Figure 8.5. First, 'things' are solid and predictable, but 'people' are not. However, we all want 'certainty' in our life; ambiguity disturbs us and our sense of control. How much better everything would be if we knew how people would react, would behave, would perform! In *Mapping Motivation*[18] we pointed out one consequence of this in organisational life: how leaders, often subconsciously, were drawn to work on finance, or marketing, or operations, because these areas were more solid and predictable;[19] unlike the people domain.

The lesson for leadership, then, is clear: the leader has to be someone who whilst rationally seeking to reduce ambiguity and uncertainty[20] in organisation life, yet realises this cannot be fully done, and so embraces the 'unknowing' that dealing with people always creates. To do this, of course, requires moral courage; it also requires the reverse of a 'know-it-all' mentality. The leader has to abandon the pretence that they know everything and that they are in charge. Of course, the buck stops with the leader, and in one obvious sense they are in charge; but if people are merely things, then leaders can learn very little from them, whereas in today's fluid and competitive environment that attitude is simply unsustainable.

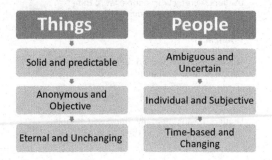

Figure 8.5 The key differences between things and people

Second, 'things' are anonymous and objective, and this has two ramifications: one, we don't feel personally involved, which means, two, we are far less likely to be subjectively hurt or disappointed. In this way we can compartmentalise our lives: go to work as if this were not our real life, and as if we saved that luxury (that is, our life) for our own free time! Thus, the leader wants – metaphorically speaking – to rub the genie's lamp. Lo! It magically happens. In the mind of the leader the employee, the people, become things; by reverse alchemy they are transmuted into things. The gold that was a person, now becomes the lead that is more useful. After all, lead is practical: we can make gutters and piping with lead and put it up everywhere; gold, on the other hand, is valuable and we need to think very carefully about how we deploy and use it, and we certainly must ensure that no gold is wasted, for it is precious. See how this reverse alchemy effects a whole attitudinal change?

Third, things are eternal[21] in the sense that they just exist without consciousness; but people inhabit time; they change.[22] That's really significant for leadership. Most people are living in the present – they have to – they have to make ends meet; indeed, many business managers and leaders[23] sometimes, often even, live almost entirely in the present, despite having been on personal development courses or been involved in strategic reviews. But for them, really, it's all about getting the job done now – exercising control, making money, demonstrating expertise. But others, a significant number, are lost souls locked into the past and all the mental baggage that it entails. So the true leader must be somebody with a long-term and future perspective. This is a defining characteristic – and that sense of the future is visionary. In other words, the leader has created the future, believes in the future before it has arrived; put even more strongly, the leader has faith. Somebody[24] once said: How can you lead somebody through a desert if you have never been there yourself? But most leaders are faced with never having done it before: Odysseus when he set sail from the ruins of Troy, or Ernest Shackleton when he arrived at the Antarctic and his ship became stuck in the ice, or Nelson Mandela when he stepped out of prison in South Africa, or Mother Teresa in the slums of Calcutta, had never been in those 'deserts' before; yet they led[25] others to freedom, empowerment and life.

The consequences, then, are understanding and embracing this 'difference' between people and things is profound. Instead of respect, we find we have systems; in place of autonomy we have processes; procedures replace empowerment; and policies stand for engagement. Instead of reality, there are substitutions – doubtless well meaning – at all levels for what we really want as humans, as people.

Effectively, 'thing' thinking becomes an all-round substitution for leading people, and the net result is that the organisation develops 'perfect' systems, processes, procedures, policies and management – at least in the mind of the senior management – and so they blindly career on, unaware of what most of their staff know: which is, that 'things' are not what they seem and that a crash is coming. Usually, of course, from staff dissatisfaction, demotivation, and disengagement.

Activity 8.7

Run a mental check now. Consider Figure 8.6. What mind-set do you have? Go through all five categories and ask, which is more important to me: the systems or the trust and respect, the processes or the autonomy of the individual, and so on. If you are unsure of the answers, then consult your people – what do they think? Figure 8.7 suggests a simple rating scale that can be used to find out how people view the organisation. Ask each individual to put an X where they think the organisation stands in terms of the balance between systems orientation and trust/respect for individuals.

This simple exercise, Figure 8.7, can be extremely insightful, especially if staff do not feel intimidated by management; of course, if they do, then there is a lot further to travel if such an organisation is going to develop real leadership capability. And it is insightful for any leader who honestly answers the questions: where am I really in terms of developing people?

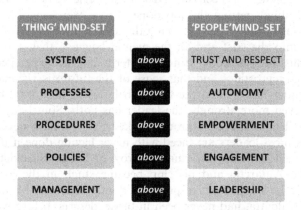

Figure 8.6 Thing versus People mind-sets

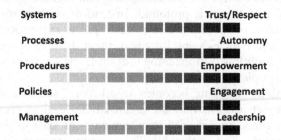

Figure 8.7 Thing/People mind-set rating scale

We have now looked at three aspects of the necessity for the leader being motivated him or herself, and for them to ensure they motivate those around them, and those whom they influence by virtue of their position. Also, we can see that understanding motivation is crucial to leadership, especially because leadership is all about envisaging and directing change – and change means things change; people change, and mapping their motivations goes exactly with the grain of working with this process.

But there is still something important missing from this picture of the leader as the motivated one and the motivator. Indeed, many have said that the number one skill of any manager or leader is in the area of recruitment, for get it wrong here, and problems multiply exponentially: leaders will always be playing catch-up. Far better to recruit the motivated and then train for skills,[26] rather than recruiting the skilful and then attempting to motivate them!

Thus, two aspects of this recruitment need exploring. First, a consideration of the role of the leader in recruitment even if they are not doing the actual interviewing and selection. This links back to our focus on leaders 'thinking' and planning. Where do we want to be? The tendency in most organisations is to fill the backstop: somebody leaves the organisation, and so we automatically replace them. But we often fail to consider one simple fact: change. The employee leaving was appointed at some point in the past, possibly a distant point, and since then things have changed. What are the actual requirements of the organisation now? And more specifically, what motivational profile is now leaving and what would – all things being equal – be the desirable motivational profile now?

This issue we considered in Chapter 7 when we looked at a major case study that Jane Thomas undertook recently. But in essence there needs to be a strategic re-evaluation of where we are, and plans made accordingly. Of course, The Five Elements planning tool we outlined in Chapters 4, 5 and 6 can be incredibly useful here.

More immediately, however we have the issue of why people are leaving our organisations in the first place. Here Motivational Maps can be eerily effective: eerily in the sense that they can often predict who is likely to leave long before that individual has expressly communicated their desire to the leader. The importance of this phenomenon can hardly be overstated: we need to recruit the best people[27] and we need to retain them; the leader is crucial in the implementation of both tasks.

Working with Motivational Maps at a senior level with a privately owned company that specialised in insuring over 80,000 properties worth in excess of £12 billion, one of the authors has a great example on staff retention. Rod Wyatt is a young senior account manager, who is highly esteemed by senior management, and thought to be top flight material. Furthermore, his particular role is mission critical to the whole organisation because although there are other 'account managers', his particular accounts contain those significant high net worth individuals which although their proportion is only 10% of the total client base, yet their revenue generation is nearly 40%. And Rod has developed a particularly strong and effective relationship with them. It took a crisis for management to wake up, belatedly, to the fact that if Rod went to a competitor organisation, then many of these clients might seek to follow with Rod. How effective would their contracts of employment be if this were to happen? And, anyway, quite apart from losing clients, there was the obvious fact that losing Rod per se would be disastrous simply in terms of the expertise and knowledge of those clients he possessed.

Motivational Maps began work with the organisation and began by mapping the motivations of the senior staff, and then all the employees. The average motivational score across the all the staff combined was 55% motivated.[28] Rod's first Motivational Map produced the following 22 numbers.

Activity 8.8

Imagine that you are Rod's boss – his leader – and your mapping motivation consultant presents you with this first map of Rod's. Leaving aside the wider context of Rod's team (of 14 staff at the time of the Map, but expanding) and other team scores, identify three key points to either feedback to Rod or action as his leader. See Figure 8.8.

The first thing to notice is that Rod (an invaluable member of staff whom we consider destined for greater things) is not as motivated as we might like. At 62% motivated we are approaching that critical point where at below 60% significant demotivation may be occurring. And this is exactly what senior management realised when they discovered this result.

Motivational Map Summary for Rod Wyatt – MONTH 1			
Motivator	Position	Score	PMA (/10)
Defender	1	26	6
Spirit	2	23	6
Searcher	3	22	7
Expert	4	21	
Builder	5	19	
Creator	6	19	
Director	7	18	
Star	8	17	
Friend	9	15	
PMA Score	62%		

Figure 8.8 Rod Wyatt's first Motivational Map

Second, the top three motivators are conflicted in that Rod wants security –
and so is risk-averse – but also wants freedom and to make a difference,
which suggests he is a risk-taker and change-maker. So, as Rod's leader we
will need to consider the balance of what we want from Rod in this role: is he
sufficiently addressing change issues, or is he playing safe with his Defender
motivator top? Given that this is an insurance company, avoiding or reducing
risk is important in terms of operational effectiveness.

Finally, Rod heads up a large team but his Director motivator is only
seventh in terms of his desires. Thus, the question must be: does he have a full
range of management and leadership skills to offset the fact that 'managing'
people is not something he really wants to do? There is, perhaps, here a
training implication.

On the basis of this Map a coach was appointed to help Rod develop further leadership skills, but it was 'sold' to him under the umbrella of enabling
him to make a bigger difference (Searcher) and to free up time (Spirit), which
he readily accepted and seemed to like.

Move on three months and the Map was done again.[29]

Activity 8.9

Study Figure 8.9 and compare and contrast it with Figure 8.8. What is surprising? What has happened? What would your response be to this Motivational Map?

Motivational Map Summary for Rod Wyatt – MONTH 4			
Motivator	Position	Score	PMA (/10)
Builder	1	26	1
Defender	2	22	3
Spirit	3	21	5
Expert	4	21	
Star	5	20	
Director	6	19	
Searcher	7	18	
Creator	8	17	
Friend	9	16	
PMA Score	22%		

Figure 8.9 Rod Wyatt's second Motivational Map

What is surprising – shocking even – is that after a significant and costly intervention Rod's motivation has dropped from 62% to 22%! The exact opposite of what management were expecting. And a further surprise is that a motivator, the Builder, that wasn't even in Rod's top three before (in fact, was ranked fifth) is now his most important motivator. Furthermore, what has also happened is that his third motivator, the Searcher, has now dropped to his seventh. This is highly significant as he is leading an account management team, and the Searcher motivator is, along with the Friend (note his lowest motivator in both Maps), widely considered to be the most customer-centric of the motivators. This means that in terms of his role Rod has almost certainly lost his 'mojo'; indeed, what has really happened seems to be that he has given up on making a difference and now wants to make money instead; but of course he is not in a direct sales commission role.

The senior management team had immediate access to these results, but for whatever reason did not think there was any cause for alarm. But we understood immediately what this meant: we told the CEO quite plainly – you need to do something, Rod is considering leaving your organisation! At first, this information was met with blank disbelief. How could he be: why, the CEO said, Rod was at a meeting yesterday and was fine, and I even spoke to him this morning (she said) and we had a pleasant exchange. Why would he want to leave; he has everything here?

Why, indeed? Speak to him. We are certain he is planning to leave, but is being highly discreet about it. Lo! And so it proved – a five-minute chat with the CEO turned into an hour-long deep conversation in which Rod confessed leaving was exactly what he intended to do. Some small incident in which he felt his merits and loyalty had been overlooked rankled with him; and furthermore, he had no idea of what we, as consultants, already knew: that he was being groomed for promotion. Their confidence in him no one had thought to relay to him, so that he actually knew it. The coaching, on the other hand, had appeared a mere sop in the absence of what was to him real recognition – as in a better, even more secure job, the Defender. In his own mind, if he couldn't get that security, then going elsewhere for money seemed a better option.

Once the CEO realised – and she did almost immediately she heard it from his mouth – she responded brilliantly well: Rod was reassured, alerted to an internal opportunity that would be coming up in the near future, and again pressed to see his coaching and more training as preparation for this new, expanded position. Crisis averted.

Three months later Rod did another Map. For the sake of convenience, we now group all three Maps together in one 'team' Map (the team of three Rods!), so the you can easily see and follow the changes.[30]

Activity 8.10

Now look at Figure 8.10 and the column for Month 7. What points emerge from looking at these numbers compared with Month 1 and Month 4? Overall, is this good progress or not? What recommendations would you make?

The results of Month 7 in Figure 8.10 are good, but clearly much more needs to be done to ensure Rod's future within the company. Once motivation takes a serious knock, as Rod's had done (and given Rod is a cautious, careful person, as should be evident from all we have said about him) it takes a lot to build it up again. But the jump from 22% to 56% is highly significant and now going in the right direction.

But more pleasing still are the small shifts that have occurred: the quest for money, The Builder, has dropped back, which is appropriate given his role; the Expert has inched up and made the top three, which is possibly a reflection of the effect the coaching and training is making on him; the Spirit has dropped out of the top three, and since that is the most mercurial of the motivators, and at odds with his Defender, that internal conflict has lessened; and note, too, the Director, as a motivator, has consistently edged up, from 18/40 to 19/40 and now 21/40. Since we have bigger leadership and management aspirations for Rod, this too is good news.

Obviously, more could be said as Maps are information and insight-rich, but for now it is enough to comment on why we have chosen this mini-case

Rod Wyatt – MONTHS 1, 4 and 7					
	Month 1	Month 4	Month 7		
Motivator	Score	Score	Score	Total	Rank
Defender	26|1	22|2	23|1	71	1
Builder	19	26|1	21	66	2
Expert	21	21	22|3	64	3
Searcher	22|3	18	22|2	62	4
Spirit	23|2	21|3	17	61	5
Director	18	19	21	58	6
Star	17	20	19	56	7
Creator	19	17	17	53	8
Friend	15	16	18	49	9
Personal Audit %	62%	22%	56%	47%	

Personal Audit Scores	Month 1	Month 4	Month 7
Score 1	6	1	5
Score 2	6	3	6
Score 3	7	5	7

Figure 8.10 Rod Wyatt's three Motivational Maps

study in mapping motivation: the leader needs to retain the best staff, and that means that the leader mustn't lose them where he or she can avoid that loss. The Maps, then, alert leaders to potential employee losses (but of course, not all) and increase the chances of an intervention which can identify what the issues are and provide mechanisms for keeping them on side.

Notes

1 "There is plenty of evidence to show that the most successful companies over the long term are those that motivate their people, train them and encourage them to come up with fresh ideas"– Matthew Lynn, Boorish Bosses are bad for Business, *Money Week*, 2 November 2018.

2 Sun Tzu, cited by Donald G Krause, *The Way of the Leader*, Nicolas Brealey (1997).

3 John Adair, *Effective Leadership Masterclass*, Pan Books (1997).

4 Not to 'walk the talk' and to be inconsistent erodes faith in leaders and leadership; Donald G. Krause has 4 more interesting 'no-nos': "There are four things an effective leader should always avoid: conjecture, bias, inflexibility, and conceit", *The Way of the Leader*, Nicolas Brealey (1997). Additionally, "to be a leader you must be yourself. You can't fake it". In other words, being genuine is the key factor of leadership. Warren Bennis, https://oreil.ly/2sbRbaT.

5 To reinforce this point, John Adair, a foremost leadership theorist, in his 'The Eight Principles of Motivation' for leaders, makes "Be Motivated Yourself" his number 1 principle. *From Leadership and Motivation*, Kogan Page (1990/ 2009).

6 For more on the lowest motivator and its implications, see *Mapping Motivation for Coaching*, James Sale and Bevis Moynan, Routledge (2018), Chapter 6.

7 "Some authors credit SWOT to Albert Humphrey, who led a convention at the Stanford Research Institute (now SRI International) in the 1960s and 1970s using data from Fortune 500 companies. However, Humphrey himself did not claim the creation of SWOT, and the origins remain obscure" – https://bit.ly/1dEoLw7.

8 For more on the correlation between Maslow's Hierarchy and the Motivational Maps, see *Mapping Motivation*, James Sale, Routledge (2016), Chapter 3.

9 We have chosen the Searcher as our focus because in an analysis of over 50,000 Maps completed, the Searcher is the most common dominant motivator.

10 Robert Greene, in his *33 Warfare Strategies of War*, Profile books (2006) gives the example of John Churchill, Duke of Marlborough, as a leader of military genius who had the "ability to stay cheerful in the face of fools" and who never let himself "get angry or frustrated" – a tendency which high idealism may often foster.

11 Job enrichment has been a constant theme since the times of Maslow and Hertzberg's original works on motivation. See Herzberg, F *et al. Job Attitudes: Reviews of Research and Opinion*, Psychological Service of Pittsburg (1957) and A. Maslow, *New Knowledge in Human Values*, Harper and Bros (1959). The key thing from our perspective is not to try to re-design work or jobs around generic motivators, but use the Motivational Maps to establish what the employees actually and really want.

12 For more on this, see *Mapping Motivation*, ibid., Chapter 5; and *Mapping Motivation for Engagement*, James Sale and Steve Jones, Routledge (2018), Chapter 1.

13 A recent analysis of this problem is from Matthew Lynn who writes: "Modern capitalism is constantly under attack for its rampant short-termism. Investors are obsessed with quarterly results. Chief executives are only interested in getting the share price up for a few months so they can collect their next massive bonus" –

"The Easy Solution to Short-termism", *Money Week*, 10 March 2017. Notice two things: how the short-termism affects the judgement and focus of the leader, the chief executive; also, it is fair to say, Lynn identifies organisations where long-termism is the norm and with spectacular success. He says, "The famous example now is Amazon, a company that obsesses over customer satisfaction, and which seems hardly to care about making a profit".

14 Paradoxically, of course, they are also our greatest source of potential pleasure and joy.

15 For a lot more on countering such limiting beliefs in one's life, read *Mapping Motivation for Coaching*, ibid. And as it applies specifically to leaders, keep in mind Richard Barrett's observation: "We are not able to become true leaders until we become authentic individuals, and we are not able to become authentic individuals until we release our unconscious fears" – *Liberating the Corporate Soul*, Routledge (1998).

16 Obviously, excellent leaders do not have this problem! There are many books on outstanding leaders in all fields. We have commented in passing on the military and the spiritual, but take exploration: Sir Ernest Shackleton was an astonishing leader. Margot Morrell and Stephanie Capparell in their book, *Shackleton's Way*, Nicolas Brealey (2001), list the qualities he had, but top of the list was 'people': "Cultivate a sense of compassion and responsibility for others. You have a bigger impact on the lives of those under you than you can imagine".

17 To reify means, as we have indicated, to materialise, or to convert mentally a concept into a thing; in other words, (if we may coin a word) to 'thing-ise' something. Where the concept is simply an abstraction, then no harm may be done. But of course where the concept is 'people', dreadful harm may ensue, as we are suggesting. Another way of expressing this is 'objectifying' people – treating them as if they were objects.

18 James Sale, *Mapping Motivation: Unlocking the key to Employee Energy and Engagement*, ibid., Chapter 1.

19 A wonderful comment that animadverts on this is: "Those who limit their benchmarks to rational and financial outcomes will go nowhere slowly", Kevin Roberts CEO worldwide Saatchi & Saatchi.

20 In Chapter 5 we talked of VUCA: "We live in a VUCA world – Volatile, Uncertain, Complex and Ambiguous – and its changing the face of business forever", Dr Alan Watkins, *Coherence*, Kogan Page (2014).

21 When we say that things are eternal what we mean is that in their nature they are: they have taken 3,000-year old honey out of a pyramid and found it still edible; and the mummies within could remain mummies forever, only the living person inside the wrappings has perished. No environment could or would make a human being immortal, but things – objects – could exist indefinitely.

22 And this is why of course that Motivational Maps is the ideal tool to chart these ambiguities; it works with change and people rather than trying to 'fix' it and them in amber, as it were.

23 As Dr Alan Watkins says: "So the challenge for most leaders is getting out of the tyranny of 'today' ". Also, "However, the greatest businesses spend as much time building the future as they do managing the present". Ibid.

24 "The great illusion of leadership is to think that others can be led out of the desert by someone who has never been there" – Henri Nouwen, *The Wounded Healer*, Darton, Longman & Todd (2014).

25 The meaning of to lead is, etymologically: to cause go along with oneself (from the Old Teutonic: 'road', 'journey').

26 Bill Taylor, "Hire for Attitude, Train for Skill", *Harvard Business Review*, 1 February 2011, https://bit.ly/2sb3aFI. We are using the words attitude and motivation interchangeably here, although they are not the same, but they both relate to those intangible elements that make for a positive contribution in the workplace.

27 This was said effectively by Leo Rosten: "First-rate people hire first-rate people; second-rate people hire third-rate people" – https://bit.ly/2R5ws7s.

28 Not the topic now, but within a year the overall motivational score for the whole company was up by 5.3% and, furthermore, there was a shift from 'Defender' as their collective top motivator – very risk averse and procedural – to Searcher, which was and proved much more client-orientated. An overall shift of over 5% in the motivational scoring is a huge difference, as the company discovered. There will be much more on these change issues in the forthcoming book, *Mapping Motivation for Strategy, Change and Innovation*, Routledge (2021).

29 At this point, since the whole organisation was going through a massive change programme, all employees were being mapped on a 3-monthly basis.

30 We have also changed the format of the team map simply for the purposes of clarity: original team maps are colour-coded, which makes them easy to read. But in using grey shading in this textbook, we thought it would be easier if we identified the top three motivators in the respective 1-, 4-, 7-month periods by using 26/1 or 22/2 to indicate the score out of 40 / followed by the ranking, first or second and so on.

Conclusion

This has been a long journey and we have repeatedly stressed that we are scarcely covering all that could be said about becoming an effective leader. But we have kept our focus on what we think is the main thing: namely, the importance of motivation not just in the delivery of effective leadership, but in its very being – its heart and soul as it were. If we recall what we said in the Introduction to this book, we will remember the four theories of leadership and most importantly, perhaps, the behavioural theories. One key of this theory was the distinction between two dimensions of behaviour: either leaders who were high in 'initiating structure' or those high in 'consideration'.

Initiating structure comes down to what we might call a task orientation, a concern or obsession with WHAT we do as an organisation. This, of course, is highly necessary, but in itself is flawed: we saw this in Chapter 7 where we encountered a leader who was pretty much obsessed with the tasks set him, and had lots of optimism and confidence and energy (motivation) initially, but soon ran into the quicksand of people from whose negative view of his performance he could not extricate himself or escape, and so failed.

For the second dimension of behavioural theory is what we called consideration; and this is about a people – employee – orientation that is relationship driven. This is about HOW we do what we do through the employees that work for us. Our treatment of them is going to have an inordinate effect on WHAT actually is achieved; and indeed, whether what is done is lasting or not. In this modern age in which we live the concept of making a difference or leaving a legacy is ubiquitous, and we think virtually impossible to do (that is, positive legacy) without the full support of our staff, our people.

Because we have focused on motivation, argued that it is more than 50% of a leader's whole responsibility to inculcate, develop and nurture, then what this book has been about has been the exploration of motivation in all aspects, as we see it, of the leader's real 'task': namely, the process of acquiring, developing and retaining the right people. If this sounds too obvious as you reach our conclusion, then we have to stress again that it is not: a very recent, and excellent in its way, global summary of leadership in 2018[1] with

25 insights into leadership for the future, only mentions the word 'motivation'[2] in one of the 25 insights!

The same paper cites research[3] from more than 2,500 HR professionals which found that 50% of organisations do not have well-integrated and strategically aligned leadership development programs or processes; 78% see their leadership career planning/pathing systems as only moderately effective or worse; and 65% do not believe their leaders have high-quality, effective development plans; and there is plenty more bad news too! For example, what they call the "The Perils of a Top-Down, Top-Only View". As Evan Sinar[4] observes:

> To gauge why few organizations succeed in cultivating potential, we looked at one of the first decisions made when creating a high-potential program: how deeply to extend it. Nearly half of organizations (46 percent) limit their potential focus to senior-most levels. Even more troubling, this percentage has barely changed from 2014 (45 percent) and reflects a costly misstep.

The point we are making here in our conclusion is that by focusing on motivation, using Motivational Maps, we must – de facto – start with the employees, so build up from the 'bottom', reverse the whole tendency to exercise a 'top-down', command and control, form of leadership. Whilst we don't disapprove of digitisation, adaptability, AI, big data, and a whole lot of other buzz-words, we have to point out that they seem to us, used in this context of effective leadership, just another way of kicking the can further down the road: investing billions of dollars and pounds into the latest fangled initiatives on which massive hopes are pinned, but which are unlikely to deliver. The only initiatives that will are those that focus, really focus, on people and their motivators;[5] there is no other way.

To consolidate this point, the Forbes Coaches Council Community last year posted their 14 Leadership Trends That Will Shape Organizations In 2018.[6] Of their 14 points, 13 of them of all about people, staff and staff development: consider the following:[7]

1 Investing In Human Capital Development
2 Increasing Emphasis On Empathetic Leadership
3 Focusing On Individual Growth
4 Leading By Actions And Examples
5 Turning Organizations Into A Truly Customer-Centric Business
6 Embracing 'Work-Life Blend'
7 Paying Attention To Internal Factors That Are In Their Control
8 Having An Objective Outsider
9 Promoting Continuous Education
10 Encouraging All Team Members To Be Brand Ambassadors

It would be tedious to demonstrate how all 13 of these trends are or can be met by using the Mapping Motivation processes outlined in this book, but if we think about three of the less obvious ones: embracing the work-life blend is clearly about leadership taking more responsibility for the well-being and wellness of their employees; further, it is about the employees bringing more energy to their work as a result of their enhanced well-being. Motivation, as we keep saying, is crucial to this purpose. Or, consider having an objective outsider: how is that relevant to motivation and Maps? In several ways: first, the same principle applies to the outsider as applies to any leader; they need to have higher levels of motivation than the staff they are advising. Second, the word 'objective' implies what the real issue is: a need for a wider perspective and an avoidance of Groupthink.[8] We have covered this in Chapters 3, 6 and 7, as we turned to the topics of 360 motivational feedback and team compositions. But here, what is to stop a Motivational Maps' profile being done on the 'objective outsider' to see how their profile matches – or not – the individuals, teams or whole organisation that they are advising? Third, proactively elevating and retaining women leaders is certainly within the remit of what Maps may help an organisation do: motivational profiles are gender neutral, non-stereotyping (since they change over time), and correlated to performance – the key issue whether one be male or female. In short, in every way one can almost think of, motivation is at the root of helping organisations solve (keeping in mind that people are never 'solved'; there is always the need to 'solve' again) long-standing, entrenched and persistent performance and engagement issues.

Jim Ware[9] said, "Your role as a leader is not to make people do what you want, it's to encourage them to want what you want". But what, we say, is what do you want? We have been here before with purpose, goals and objectives and the whole cascading of 'tasks' on the back end of these admirable and necessary aims. What if, though, the leader before asking him or herself what it is that they have to do – the task – they ask, what do I want? What are my energies, in which direction are they facing, and do they help or hinder me in the achievement of the organisational goals I am inheriting or about to formulate? How much more powerful would that be? We talk about this a lot in *Mapping Motivation for Engagement*[10] where we suggest that instead of considering motivation as the last factor in performance, behind Direction and Skills/knowledge, we place it first instead. Our motivation is quintessentially what we want.

Thus, truly we can say we understand (as leaders) what we want first, and primary to what we want is understanding our motivations. Only then can we begin to understand what our staff want and start that short or long process –

depending on context – which enables employees to begin to want what we want. And, of course, they begin to want what you want when you consistently give them what they want! It is a bizarre but true paradox.

The nine motivators of Motivational Maps are an awesome way to understand what people want, and furthermore to the perceptive leader they show the way to get people to want to transform. This comes down to something we have covered in all the books on Mapping Motivation so far, but will be saying a lot more about in the future volumes in this series: namely, Reward Strategies.

Every Map – individual, youth, team or organisational – comes with its own built-in menu of rewards based on the relevant profile. But the nine motivators are generic in nature, which means that the leader has an endless number of ways he can influence staff simply, in the first place, by using the appropriate motivational language to describe what is happening, and then by providing commensurate rewards based on their profiles. Without manipulation, it is giving staff what they want, and sure as eggs are eggs when you do that they become highly responsive to giving you – the leader – what you want.

Ultimately between leader and led there has to be a dance. This returns us to Chapter 1 when we talked about metaphors for leadership: 'play' was one of them. Well, dancing is a specialised form of play, and if we want to lead – indeed, if we want any kind of meaningful relationship with anybody else – we have to dance. That means working in step together, mirroring each other's movements, paying attention to the whole body language of the other person and responding appropriately to their movements, including their – and sometimes our own – missteps. When that happens, we take corrective action; we don't 'beat' our dancing partner up to prove who's in charge; at least we don't if want the grace, the symmetry and joie de vivre of a delightful dance. In business terms that means, we don't 'beat people up' if we wish to enjoy high performance and productivity, resulting profits, and final pre-eminence in our field. No, we get to understand them at a motivational level. Remember, as Dr Alan Watkins[11] put it: "It's a general principle that all positive emotion is transformative". Yes, the very thing we wanted in our Introduction: not mere transactional leadership but transformational leaders.

So it is we come to commend this process of Mapping Motivation to you: we believe that if you take on board the whole leadership and motivation agenda, along with some of the techniques and tools, that we have outlined in this book for your employees, you will be able to achieve far more than you ever thought possible in the work place. In one sense, compared with many of the latest technology-type solutions to employee issues, this is simple. But as we said in our Introduction, and still believe, quoting D. G. Krause[12] who expressed it in his *The Way of the Leader* – a summation of the ancient wisdom and principles of Sun Tzu and Confucius – "Only what is simple can produce outstanding success".

The first step, then, for developing your leadership capabilities, as we conclude is: make sure you do your own Motivational Map, so go to endnote 21 in the Preface to access how to.

Notes

1 See Global Leadership Forecast 2018: *25 Research Insights to Fuel your People Strategy*, Development Dimensions International, Inc., The Conference 1 Board Inc., EYGM Limited – https://bit.ly/2EUH6nA. They also say: "We've followed perceptions of leadership capability over the years that indicate organizations' progress in building stronger leadership capability. Are they improving? Despite billions spent on leadership development annually, the answer, yet again, is no". Which is good, but looking at some of their priorities in improving leadership capability we return to our central point of motivation. They outline (conceding that not every competency has the same impact) six points of focus under the heading: Where Should You Focus? The foci are: Lead with digitisation; Adaptability; Execution; Hyper-collaboration; Identify and develop new talent; and a 360° view. Clearly, this all sounds exciting, but we have to ask whether 'hyper-collaboration' is merely team work on steroids! Execution might be our old-fashioned 'Doing' as per the '4+1' model and The Five Elements process. As for 360°, we believe this book provides a unique insight into where and how this applies. But whether their number one focus, Leading with digitisation, is right we are sure context will determine. But from our perspective this can seem very much like a way of automating the 'top-down' approach that we – and nearly all research – claim doesn't work.
2 Indeed, the paper, *Global Leadership Forecast 2018*, ibid., is 68 pages long and only Richard Wellins (one of 12 authors) uses the word 'motivation' (ten times in total). Since the research is designed for aspiring leaders all the way to the C-Suite, we find this very concerning: 11 thought-leaders on leadership seem to think that motivation is unimportant to the future of leadership.
3 Rebecca L Ray, ibid., also citing Mitchell, C, Ray, R L, and van Ark, B (January 2017), The Conference Board *CEO Challenge® 2017: Leading Through Risk, Disruption and Transformation*, New York, The Conference Board, https://bit.ly/2EUH6nA.
4 Evan Sinar, *Rethinking Leadership Potential: Why Broader Is Better*, Global Leadership Forecast 2018: *25 Research Insights to Fuel your People Strategy*, ibid.
5 And to be clear here: we are not saying that the only solution is using Motivational Maps. There are other excellent people-type tools and processes, but the focus has to be on how we address people and the process of interacting with them.
6 See *14 Leadership Trends That Will Shape Organizations In 2018*, https://bit.ly/2t6gEmK.
7 The 14th trend is Taking A Stand On Social And Political Issues, which is too about people, but really outside the remit of this book, although clearly certain issues will appeal more to certain motivators than others; 14 Leadership Trends, ibid.
8 For more on Groupthink see James Sale, *Mapping Motivation*, Routledge (2016) and James Sale and Bevis Moynan, *Mapping Motivation for Coaching*, Routledge (2018).
9 Jim Ware, *Leadership: What's New* (July, 2015), https://bit.ly/2GtzVXd.
10 James Sale and Steve Jones, *Mapping Motivation for Engagement*, Routledge (2018), Chapter 3.
11 Dr Alan Watkins, *Coherence*, Kogan Page (2014).
12 Donald G Krause, *The Way of the Leader*, Nicholas Brealey (1997).

Resources

This section of the book is designed to help you find more information about motivation, engagement and Motivational Maps. It is not comprehensive and will be subsequently updated.

Information about Motivation Maps Ltd and Motivational Maps

Motivational Maps Ltd was founded in 2006. Its Motivational Map is ISO accredited: ISO 17065: http://www.irqao.com/PDF/C11364-51147.pdf.

The company website can be found at www.motivationalmaps.com and enquiries should be addressed to info@motivationalmaps.com.

James Sale, the author, can be found at www.jamessale.co.uk, Dorset, UK and his LinkedIn profile is: https://uk.linkedin.com/in/jamesmotivationsale.

Jane Thomas, the co-author and Senior Map Practitioner, can be found at: www.premierlifeskills.co.uk, Dorset, UK and her LinkedIn profile is: https://linkedin.com/in/janepremierlifeskills.

For more information on how to become an Accredited Mapping Motivation for Leadership consultant contact Jane Thomas – jane@premierlifeskills.co.uk.

There are currently four different Motivational Maps available:

1 The Motivational Map is for individuals and employees to discover what motivates them and how motivated they are; this produces a 15-page report on the individual.
2 The Motivational Team Map, which the forthcoming book, *Mapping Motivation for Innovation, Strategy and Change* (Routledge, 2021) is largely devoted to. This is a 22+ page report which synthesises the individual maps from any number of people, and reveals what the overall motivational scores are. It is ideal for team leaders and managers.
3 The Motivational Organizational Map produces a 44-page report and synthesises the information from any number of team maps be they from the whole organization or a section of the whole organization. Ideal for senior managers to understand how to implement their strategies through

people. In 2021 Routledge will release *Mapping Motivation for Innovation, Strategy and Change*, which will cover aspects of this diagnostic.

4   The Motivational Youth Map is different from the other Maps in that it has three outputs: one for the student, one for the teacher and one for the parent; all designed to help motivate the student to succeed at school and college. Ideal for 11–18 year olds and school and colleges looking to motivate their students. There is also the Youth Group Map.

The Motivational Map questionnaire is in nine different languages: English, Hungarian, Spanish, German, French, Italian, Greek, Lithuanian, and Portuguese.

Motivational Maps Ltd has licensed over 500 consultants, coaches and trainers to deliver the Map products in 14 countries. There are 5 Senior Practitioners of Maps in the UK:

UK Senior Practitioners

Bevis Moynan, Magenta Coaching Solutions, www.magentac.co.uk, Cambridgeshire
Carole Gaskell, Full Potential Group, https://www.fullpotentialgroup.co.uk, London
Kate Turner, Motivational Leadership, www.motivationalleadership.co.uk, Wiltshire
Susannah Brade-Waring, Aspirin Business Solutions, www.aspirinbusiness.com, Dorset

Motivational Maps resources can be found on www.motivationalmaps.com/Resources
For more information on Motivational Youth Maps contact Mark Turner at www.motivationalmapseducation.com and mark@motivationalmentoring.com.

Other key books on motivation, engagement and personal development

Twelve books we like on motivation, leadership, and related topics are:

The 33 Strategies of War, Robert Greene, Profile Books (2006)
The Chimp Paradox, Dr Steve Peters, Vermillion (2012)
Coherence, Dr Alan Watkins, Kogan Page (2014)
The Future of Management, Gary Hamel, Harvard Business School Press (2007)
Insights into Liberating Leadership, Ali Stewart, ReThink Press (2015)
Introducing Leadership, David Pardy, Routledge (2006)

Leadership and Motivation, John Adair, Kogan Page (1990/2006)
Leading Beyond the Ego, edited by John Knights, Routledge (2018)
Shackleton's Way, Margot Morrell and Stephanie Capparell, Nicolas Brealey (2001)
Thick Face, Black Heart, Chin-Ning Chu, Nicolas Brealey (1997)
Victory! Brian Tracy, TarcherPerigee (2002/2017)
The Way of the Leader, Donald G Krause, Nicolas Brealey (1997)

Index